T0355795

Praise for *Culture Matters* . . .

Jenni Catron has a real gift for simplifying the complex topic of organizational culture. *Culture Matters* is a powerful framework you can use to shape a healthy culture. This is a must-read for any leader who is looking to boost team engagement and make a lasting impact.

> —John C. Maxwell, *New York Times* Bestselling
> Author and Founder of Maxwell Leadership

For far too long, countless leaders around the world have wanted to build an extraordinary culture. They just didn't know how. In *Culture Matters*, Jenni has pulled back the curtain on the mission-critical task of culture craft. What she has revealed will be life-giving, soul-enriching, and performance-enhancing for your team and your organization.

> —Mark Miller, *Wall Street Journal* and International
> Bestselling Author of *Culture Rules* and Former
> VP of High Performance Leadership
> at Chick-fil-A, Inc.

We all recognize a healthy culture when we see it—teams are motivated, energized, engaged, and fully committed. Likewise, we all know a bad culture—teams lack motivation, are drained of energy, and are always looking for an escape. Healthy cultures don't just happen; they require work and a plan, which is why *Culture Matters* is such a must-read for leaders. In it Jenni Catron has given us the practical strategies necessary for building a culture we all desire—a culture of trust, transparency, and collaboration.

> —David Ashcraft, President and CEO,
> Global Leadership Network,
> Author of *What Was I Thinking?*

I could not be more excited about the relevancy of Jenni Catron's latest book, *Culture Matters*. Once again, she draws from her extensive leadership experiences and years of consultancy. She systematically delivers the LeadCulture Framework, designed to transform your organizational culture. Jenni's genius is her methodology and practical application. Today is the day to buy this book. Take it one step at a time and watch your team grow, thrive, and become *truly* unstoppable!

— Tami Heim, President and CEO of
  Christian Leadership Alliance

Jenni Catron has proven over and over that her wisdom around culture building in the ministry and workplace improves and shapes the lives of teams—leaders and employees alike. *Culture Matters* is the book every leader needs to read if you want to retain good team members, stay on mission, and impact as many people as possible with your work.

— Annie F. Downs, *New York Times*
  Bestselling Author of *That Sounds Fun*

Jenni Catron reminds us that culture is not just a side project for leaders; it's the foundation upon which great teams are built. Her practical insights and the LeadCulture Framework provide leaders with the tools they need to shape environments where trust, clarity, and engagement flourish. This is a guide for any leader who wants to unlock the full potential of their team.

— Matt Randerson, Vice President,
  Growth, Barna Group

As a fellow executive who has witnessed firsthand the profound impact of leadership on organizational culture, I am thrilled to endorse *Culture Matters* by Jenni Catron. Jenni's deep understanding of what it takes to cultivate a thriving, unstoppable team is unparalleled. Her insights are not only practical but deeply rooted in years of experience leading high-performing teams as well.

This book is a must-read for any leader committed to fostering a positive, productive, and resilient organizational environment. Jenni's wisdom and expertise shine through on every page, making this a valuable resource for anyone looking to elevate their team and, ultimately, their entire organization.

—Tricia Sciortino, CEO of BELAY

Most leaders have only the fuzziest of ideas about what *culture* really means in their organization. And those leaders who do have a very clear idea of what they want their culture to be are almost always projecting a subjective mishmash of their own preconceptions and preferences.

When I first listened as Jenni Catron shared the acutely observed, right-on-the-button LeadCulture Framework outlined in this immensely readable book, I knew instantly that here was the rigorous, comprehensive, flexible, and above all implementable model that every previous book on the topic had missed.

If you don't think culture is important for your organization's success, you desperately need to read this book. If you do think culture is important, you'll devour it.

—Les McKeown, Founder and
CEO, Predictable Success

I thought I understood team culture well. Then I read this book and realized I only understood a fraction of it. Jenni Catron gives a master class in team and organizational culture. Even if you think you have a great culture, there is so much to learn here. Every founder, boss, and manager needs to read this."

—Carey Nieuwhof, Author, Podcaster, Speaker

Jenni Catron, in her timely book *Culture Matters,* has provided an effective template to equip leaders of any type of organization on how to proactively develop a culture to galvanize optimal success. This book provides a compelling reminder that a positive team culture is never accidental but is dependent upon the leader's commitment and skills to connect people to purpose. Jenni's exquisite writing style enables this seminal leadership book to be not only informative, but also refreshingly enjoyable and memorable.

—Dr. Kent Schlichtemeier, Director of the Servant
Leadership Institute at Concordia University Irvine.

In *Culture Matters,* Jenni Catron offers a comprehensive blueprint for creating and growing organizational culture. This guide is essential for any leader committed to elevating their workplace environment. Culture truly matters, and this book is a phenomenal resource for fostering growth and success. As a recognized culture expert, Jenni Catron shares her decades of experience to help you focus on what matters most."

—Dee Ann Turner, 3x Bestselling Author,
International Keynote Speaker,
Vice President, Talent, Chick-fil-A (retired)

Jenni Catron has written the playbook on building culture! This book shares practical insights and strategies for maintaining and growing a strong and healthy culture backed by Jenni's extensive knowledge and experience on the topic. This book is a must-read and a homerun for leaders at any stage or level of leadership!

—Jordan Montgomery, Bestselling Author
of *The Art of Encouragement*

This book provides a comprehensive and practical roadmap for leaders who aspire to cultivate an unstoppable team culture. Jenni's insights into the significance of organizational clarity, psychological safety, and personal fulfillment are game-changing. The LeadCulture Framework is not just theoretical but also filled with actionable steps that any leader can implement to see tangible improvements in their team's dynamics.

Culture Matters is more than just a guide; it's a call to action for leaders serious about making a lasting impact. If you are ready to invest in your team and transform your organizational culture, this book is essential."

—Rich Birch, Founder, unSeminary
and Church Growth Coach

"Dad, do you think I could meet Jenni Catron?" my daughter Jesse asked me. What a gift to me as a Dad to be able to introduce my daughter to a leader and friend I've admired and respected for years. Jenni knows how to create thriving organizations that are built upon a healthy culture. Now, her framework is available to us all."

—Jeff Henderson, Executive Director of Leadership
Innovation and Strategy, Chick-fil-A, Inc.

This book is filled with invaluable insights and timeless wisdom. More than just a guide on culture, it serves as a blueprint for business success. It offers a clear lens to reflect on past mistakes while providing a sharp focus on the organizational needs of the future. Follow Jenni's guide, and your business and organization will thrive!"

—JuneAn Lanigan, Partner, Development
and Business Management, WellSpring

I don't know of a more knowledgeable or experienced leader when it comes to helping organizations have a healthy and thriving culture. When I was leading an organization out of trauma and toxicity, Jenni Catron is the person I called to help me put together a plan. Now she's put her amazing framework in a book for every leader. *Culture Matters* is a game changer for any leader concerned with organization health.

—Tim Stevens, CEO and Founder, LeadingSmart

I have known Jenni for almost twenty years, and she is hands down THE leading voice in building a culture that will move your organization forward and keep your people healthy. In *Culture Matters*, Jenni uses her expertise and experiences to craft a simple yet powerful formula that's easy for everyone on your team to understand and implement. I cannot recommend Jenni and this book highly enough!

—Kadi Cole, Leadership Consultant,
Executive Coach, Author, Speaker

Jenni Catron's *Culture Matters* is a must-read for leaders looking to prioritize organizational culture. With her LeadCulture Framework, Jenni emphasizes the need to assess, define, build, equip, and commit to cultivating a healthy workplace culture. Her methodical approach, from clarifying mission and values to equipping leaders with essential skills, reflects a deep commitment to culture as a foundational leadership issue. This book is an invaluable guide for leaders seeking lasting impact through a people-centered approach.

—Jim Sheppard, CEO and Principal of Generis

CULTURE
MATTERS

CULTURE MATTERS

A FRAMEWORK FOR HELPING YOUR TEAM GROW, THRIVE, AND BE UNSTOPPABLE

BY JENNI CATRON

MAXWELL
LEADERSHIP.

Published by Maxwell Leadership Publishing, an imprint of Forefront Books, Nashville, Tennessee.
Distributed by Simon & Schuster.

Library of Congress Control Number: 2024916901

Print ISBN: 979-8-88710-036-4
E-book ISBN: 979-8-88710-037-1

Cover Design by Bruce Gore, Gore Studio, Inc.
Interior Design by PerfecType, Nashville, TN

Printed in the United States of America

Dedication

To the amazing individuals who have been on teams
I've led through the years and were subject to all my
culture-shaping experiments: Thank you for giving me the
grace to learn to lead. It's because of you that I love the sacred
work of leadership and the stewardship of team culture.

CONTENTS

FOREWORD

What makes an organization successful?

This is a question I've received countless times through my two decades of developing leaders and teams around the world. Of course, there are many characteristics we can highlight about organizations that achieve great success. But there is one characteristic that rises above the rest: culture.

Culture! Let me say it this way—if you and I were sitting across the table right now discussing the organization you lead, one of the first things out of my mouth would be, "Tell me about your culture." What do people experience when they interact with your team, your brand, your company?

There is transformative power in a strong, intentional culture.

The longer I lead, the more I come to realize that success isn't merely about achieving goals—it's about creating environments where individuals can grow, thrive, and ultimately become the best versions of themselves. And at the heart of any thriving organization lies a healthy culture.

In *Culture Matters*, Jenni Catron offers a compelling vision of what's possible when leaders make culture a strategic priority. Drawing from her own experiences as a leadership consultant and author, Jenni provides a roadmap for cultivating a culture of excellence—one where you will walk away empowered to contribute your unique talents and perspectives to a shared vision.

I love how Jenni has given us practical strategies for building a culture of trust, transparency, and collaboration. From defining core values to fostering open communication and accountability, Jenni equips leaders with the tools they need to create environments where teams not only survive but thrive.

As the CEO of Maxwell Leadership, I've had the privilege of working with leaders from a wide range of industries and backgrounds. And time and time again, I've seen the transformative power of culture in action. It's what sets exceptional organizations apart from the rest. It's the secret sauce! A healthy culture fuels innovation, fosters resilience, and ultimately drives sustainable growth.

But perhaps what I love most about *Culture Matters* is its emphasis on personal leadership. Jenni reminds us that culture isn't just something that happens at the organizational level—it starts with each one of us. As leaders, we have a responsibility to model the behaviors and values we wish to see reflected in our teams and organizations. And good leadership creates a ripple effect that extends far beyond our own teams.

I want to encourage you to embrace the principles outlined in these pages. Will you commit yourself to building a culture that reflects the very best of who you are and what you stand for? You can be a part of the solution, because building a healthy culture truly does start with you.

Always remember, true leadership begins not with a title or a position, but with a commitment to creating environments where everyone has the opportunity to thrive.

Together, let's harness the power of culture to create a future where teams are not just successful, but they are unstoppable. Because everyone deserves to be led well.

Mark Cole
CEO, Maxwell Leadership

INTRODUCTION
Culture Matters

"Culture isn't just one aspect of the game;
it is the game. In the end, an organization
is nothing more than the collective capacity of its people to create value."

—**Lou Gerstner**[1]

I f you had asked me twenty-five years ago what I'd be writing about today, I feel pretty confident I would *not* have
exclaimed, "Team culture!" Truth is, I've always enjoyed
being a lone ranger. I can count on myself. If I want something done right, I trust myself to do it. I like to move fast,
and I like to work independently. I was a shy kid who preferred to explore the neighborhood on my own or get lost
in a good book. I believed that I didn't need others. Other
people slowed me down. I was generally impatient. (In

fact, when I was nine years old, my dad gave me a lecture on needing to be more patient. Why in the world would a nine-year-old be in such a hurry?)

For the first couple of decades of my life I operated as if people were a problem to manage—a necessary evil, if you will. A means to an end. That end being whatever goal I had in my sights.

Fast-forward to today, and I absolutely believe that people *are* the point. Visions are inspiring. Goals are motivating. Accomplishments are exhilarating. But none of them are meaningful and worthwhile without the people that are a part of them.

People are the point.

Whatever dream you're chasing, whatever goal you're pursuing, I promise you won't get far unless you have a team aligned around that goal, unified in purpose, and committed to one another.

If you've experienced this, you know what I mean.

I wouldn't have believed it until I was a part of it.

In full disclosure, I was ruined early on. My first two work experiences were stark contrasts in team culture.

Growing up in the Northwoods of Wisconsin, extremes are familiar. The brutally cold winters give way (eventually) to gorgeous summers where every hot minute possible is lived on the lake. Tourists from the cities south of us flock "up north" for an escape to their summer cabins. Summers in Wisconsin are truly divine.

My first official job was at the local ice cream shop. Think small-town, mom-and-pop bungalow that serves the best ice cream in the state. Happy customers, fun coworkers, all the ice cream we could eat, and an owner who was my biggest cheerleader. My summers at the ice cream shop were some of the best days of my life.

A few months later, the tourists would head back home, the leaves would begin to turn their hints of yellow and red, and we'd close the ice cream shop for another season.

My next seasonal job was at the local Christmas tree farm. I spent my weekends making Christmas wreaths in a cold metal shed with a handful of cranky ladies who blasted terrible music from the 1970s as they complained about every detail of their life. All the while being watched like a hawk and barked at by the owner—who seemed equally miserable herself—when I made a mistake. My winters at the Christmas tree farm were some of the worst days of my life.

As I reflect on those two experiences, I realize they have some similarities. Both jobs required manual labor (if you've scooped ice cream for an extended amount of time, you know that the coveted "ice cream arm" is well earned). In both cases we produced products that customers loved— who doesn't love ice cream on a hot summer day or a beautiful Christmas wreath for the front door?

The difference in the scenarios had everything to do with the people, and the environment they created.

As I've worked with teams of all sizes and organizations of all types, I'm 100 percent confident that it would be completely possible for my experiences to be reversed. At the ice cream shop, I could just as easily say that the customers were demanding and cranky, my arm was sore from scooping ice cream for hours, my back ached from carrying ten-gallon buckets, my coworkers were competitive and snarky, and the owner was demanding and demeaning.

On the other hand, at the Christmas tree farm, the nostalgic scent of freshly clipped evergreen boughs filled the air while an amazing group of women thoughtfully and enthusiastically assembled wreaths as we belted out Christmas carols and drank hot cider to keep us warm.

Either scenario could be true.

The difference?

Culture.

Culture is the differentiator.

It's what makes any job engaging or intolerable.

It's what draws out the best or worst in us.

It's what energizes and engages or what diminishes and discourages.

As Matthew Kelly says in his book *The Culture Solution*, "Culture . . . is the ultimate competitive advantage of our age."[2]

6 REASONS TO BE INTENTIONAL ABOUT CULTURE

As we get started, let me share six reasons you should be intentional about your culture now more than ever.

1. The work you do really is all *about* people and *for* people. No matter what type of organization you're

a part of, whether you provide a service or deliver a product, people are a part of the equation. The first group of people we're responsible for is our staff. How we treat them directly impacts how they serve our customers.

2. Purpose matters more than ever. Great cultures are built on a clear sense of purpose. Employees want to know that what they are doing matters. I think this has been important to every generation of leaders, but Millennials and Gen Zers, unlike their predecessors, are willing to sacrifice income and some luxuries to be a part of something with meaning. If you don't connect people to purpose, you'll lose them.

3. Remote work is here to stay. This dynamic is radically impacting team culture. In the past, culture was often easier to "catch" because everyone clocked in and clocked out at the same time every day. We shared space in a sea of cubicles and the break room was where friendships and alliances were formed. Culture was shaped at the water cooler. With the advent of flexible schedules and remote work, the responsibility is even greater for us to define and create a consistent culture.

4. Longevity pays off. The average worker today stays just four years in a job, and this stat has been on the decline for younger workers. In order to attract and retain great people (and save the money that the revolving door costs your organization), you must create a culture that compels them to stay.

5. Navigating change requires great culture. The pace of change is faster than ever before. This means your team needs to be able to react and respond quickly. Strong cultures are nimbler. Because they trust one another, they can move more quickly together.

6. Great culture multiplies. As you create great culture with your team, they in turn will create great culture with their teams. As goes the leader, so goes the team. You need to intentionally build what you want to reproduce.

WHO WE ARE AND HOW WE WORK TOGETHER

Skim the cover stories of *Harvard Business Review* or *Forbes* magazine and you'll quickly find a plethora of articles devoted to the importance of workplace culture and why you as the leader need to be attending to it.

Culture has become the corporate buzzword of the day, and for good reason. People are what it's all about. As artificial intelligence and automation contribute to a rapidly changing workplace, the importance of stewarding our human resources is more critical than ever. But the question that haunts those of us who need to lead culture is, "What is it exactly?" In some ways, everything feels like culture—and to a great degree, that is true.

As we explore what culture is, I want to share a couple of my favorite definitions:

"Culture is a set of living relationships working toward a shared goal." Daniel Coyle, *The Culture Code*[3]

"A remarkable culture is a place where people believe the best in one another, want the best for one another, and expect the best from one another." Dr. Randy Ross, *Relationomics*[4]

My definition of culture is: Who we are and how we work together to achieve our mission.

It's simple, and it's a lot.

- *Who we are*: our purpose combined with the things that are unique and distinct to our team.
- *How we work together*: the values, beliefs, and behaviors that guide us.

Who you are is different from another organization across town.

How you work together may be radically different from the business next door.

And your mission is unique to you as well.

My definition of culture is:
Who we are and how we work
together to achieve our mission.

That's the beauty of culture. It's distinct and unique. The problem is that when culture is left undefined, every person on your team creates their own definition and lives it out in a different way.

More important than a definition is the truth that great culture doesn't happen by accident, and that's what I want you to be aware of. Your culture matters, and you as the leader are responsible for it.

Great culture is not hard to spot. Think of your favorite places to shop, your favorite brands and products, your favorite places to relax and hang out. Odds are these products and environments have something in common—they engage you. It could be the energy, the atmosphere, the quality, attitudes of the people, or any combination.

The culture of your organization matters. It matters for the people you are trying to reach. It matters for the people you are trying to lead, whether they are staff or volunteers. And frankly it matters to you. Your life is too sacred to squander in an organization that drains the life out of you.

The environment you create in your organization is either attracting or repelling. It's either building or eroding. As leaders, we set the tone for the culture. We have to own it. We have to steward it. We have to set it and we have to maintain it.

Culture building is some of the most important work you will do as a leader, but oftentimes it's the thing we take the most for granted. Plagued by goals to achieve, staff to manage, programs to run, and board members to make happy, the last thing we have time for is the proverbial "fluffy" stuff.

We are entering an era of leadership that makes culture more important than ever. Employees are eager to be a part of cultures that align with their values and beliefs. They don't want to just work to make a living; they want to work to make a difference. In today's culture, work and life collide like never before. Our entire world is at our fingertips, and we are connected and available to one another all the time. While there are certainly some downsides to our hyperconnectedness, this is our new reality. As such, it stands to reason that if our worlds are so integrated, we better make sure they are worlds we really want to be a part of.

Culture matters. In strong cultures you're motivated, energized, engaged, and fully committed. In bad cultures you lack motivation, are drained of energy, are disengaged, and are always looking for an escape.

Why do I believe this so deeply?

I've lived it. I've seen it. Done well and done poorly.

For the better part of the last twenty-five years, I've been studying great teams seeking to understand what makes them great. I've experimented with the teams I've led trying to figure out what works. Those learnings have become the LeadCulture Framework™ that I now use to help leaders of organizations of all sizes develop a thriving team so they can accelerate growth and build unstoppable momentum.

WHAT DO YOU ENVISION?

Imagine a world where your mission and vision are clear, and you have a team of employees who are energized to come to work, enjoy working together, and have clarity for how to achieve their goals.

I suspect that's the culture you aspire to. But let's talk about reality for a minute. Most days the whirlwind of busywork distracts us from our mission. If we have values, they rarely get our time or attention. We're often refereeing tension between team members. We wonder how we actually get anything done but we have this sinking feeling we could be doing more or better.

In the whirlwind of activity that demands our time as leaders, one of the things that rarely gets our attention is the intentional development of our culture. It's not a question of whether you have a culture—you do. It's a question of whether you are creating the culture you want. You don't simply drift toward extraordinary culture. It takes time, attention, and commitment. But the momentum created by intentional culture-shaping catapults you to achieving your mission with greater joy, clarity, and effectiveness.

In this book, I will walk you through the process I've developed over the last twenty-five years.

We'll cover the five key phases of the LeadCulture Framework and explore the steps to take to build your culture plan.

THE 5 PHASES OF THE LEADCULTURE FRAMEWORK:

1. **Assess**
   In this phase you'll answer the question, "Where are we now?" In order to build a pathway for the culture you aspire to, you'll need to have a clear understanding of what is true about your culture right now.

2. **Define**
   The definition phase is about dreaming. It's about answering the question, "Who are we and how do we want to work together to achieve our mission?"

You'll paint the picture of the preferred future for your team.

3. **Build**

   In the build phase you'll answer the question, "What will it take?" Now that you've defined where you are and clarified where you want to be, it's time to build a plan to close the gap between your actual and aspirational culture. In this phase you'll define the values that will guide you, the systems to support you, and the rhythms that reinforce your culture every day.

4. **Equip**

   The fourth phase is about identifying your immediate and long-term commitment to developing leaders at all levels of the organization to ensure they are equipped to lead your culture. You'll address the question, "How will we lead culture effectively?"

5. **Commit**

   The final phase is about instilling your commitment to the plan you've designed. You'll answer the question, "How do we maintain momentum?"

A NOTE ABOUT FORMAT

As you read through the book, I'll be sharing the story of my friend Steve Warren and how I led his organization through the LeadCulture Framework. (While their story is true, the names of individuals and the organization have been changed.) As I share their story, I'll be equipping you to learn and apply the framework. You will be prompted to identify a Culture Champion and build a Culture Team to help you facilitate this work most effectively.

Throughout the chapters you'll find:

- Culture Team Action Plans with instructions for how to facilitate each part of the process
- Clarity Checks, which are questions at the end of each chapter that help you take a quick assessment of what needs your attention
- Additional resources for you to download to help you implement the framework

I'm so thrilled you've picked up this book. I promise that if you'll engage this content and implement the practices I prescribe, you will see a change in your culture. And while this work takes time, the results will come if you do the work. You have to make the commitment.

My goal with this book is to equip you with the perspective you need and the framework that will help you intentionally design a growing, thriving, and unstoppable culture. I'll help you build a scalable system in which your defined organizational culture can flourish.

Attending to the culture of your team is your greatest priority as a leader. Throughout this book I'll be making the case for why I believe this is true and I'll be equipping you to take the process that my team and I use to help leaders build great culture and put it to work in your organization.

And most importantly you'll experience the absolute joy of building a team that you love working with.

Research tells us that a strong and healthy culture leads to greater employee engagement and more growth for your organization. And yet, while 90 percent of leaders believe that an engagement strategy will have an impact on their success, only 25 percent of them actually have a plan.[5]

This book is designed to help you build that plan.

1

The Power of Culture

"You can have all the right strategies in the world; if you don't have the right culture, you're dead."

—Patrick Whitesell[6]

The community I live in was settled on the banks of the Fox River in northeastern Wisconsin. In the 1700s, this area was still largely undeveloped and sparsely populated. In the 1800s, loggers discovered the valuable forests of the north woods and found a critical resource in the power of the Fox River to transport lumber further south to major cities like Milwaukee and Chicago. By the mid- to late 1800s, word had spread to the East Coast about the infamous power of the Fox River. Papermaking was a fast-growing industry and several opportunistic entrepreneurs discovered that the conditions of the Fox River were especially perfect for the force of power needed to run paper mills. Shortly thereafter the Fox Valley became home to paper barons and transformed into a vibrant hub of industry for generations to come.

Why the history lesson?

What was critical to the success of the papermaking industry was identifying the right conditions to accomplish their mission of mass-producing paper. In this case, the current of the Fox River was ideal for what they needed to do, so much so that people like the Gilberts (who owned the home that I now live in) moved their families from Pennsylvania to Wisconsin to find the right conditions.

How does this connect to culture?

To achieve your mission, the conditions matter. As a leader, you have to create the climate that will most effectively help you achieve your mission. You have to choose the environment to immerse your team in. Culture flows through everything you do. In essence, the culture of your organization is the river that is carrying your mission forward. Is your culture a stagnant pond, a slow trickle, or a rushing river? Are there dry spots in your riverbed? Are people lazily floating along, drowning in the current, or confidently navigating the waters of your culture?

Okay, maybe I'm overworking the analogy a bit, but my hope is to help you comprehend the importance of culture. Your culture carries your mission. If you are passionate about achieving the mission, vision, and goals of your organization, getting intentional about culture is essential.

Several years ago, I was recruited to an organization to help chart the vision for the future that the senior leader had defined. This organization had gone through some significant changes and there was great hope for a new vision and direction. I was compelled by the opportunity and after thoughtful evaluation accepted the job. Unfortunately, what I quickly discovered is that we were trying to drive a speedboat through a stagnant pond. We had an extraordinary mission and vision for the future but a culture that wasn't ready for it.

You can have a great vision. You can be a phenomenal leader. But if you don't understand and value the significance of the culture, your greatest vision and your best leadership are only going to get stuck in the muck of poor culture.

The environment we work in matters. The people we work with matters. So why do so many leaders struggle to build thriving cultures? Why are employees leaving faster than we can hire them? Why do those who stay seem to be working against us rather than working with us?

A key part of the problem with analyzing organizational culture is that we don't fully understand its place in the success of our organization. For many, culture seems like a luxury we'll get to when we have margin for it. We confuse culture with employee perks that feel frivolous and nonessential. Frankly, we don't understand culture's place and purpose and therefore we relegate it to a function of the human resources department and underestimate its role in being the current that carries our mission.

The challenge of making culture a priority is not an uncommon one. As leaders, we are expected to focus on vision and strategy. We don't have the luxury of cultivating kumbaya moments. The demands of investors, donors, sales targets, and growth metrics create an urgency to focus on the tactics that will help us meet these unending expectations. And yet, for all your focus and intentionality, you will hit a point where your strategy just isn't working. No matter how powerful the vision, it feels like you're operating in quicksand. You've heeded all the best practices and gone to all the right conferences, but you still feel like you're struggling to get traction toward accomplishing your vision.

There is nothing more frustrating as a leader than to have a vision burning in your heart but the inability to see that vision become reality.

We are wired to grow things. I don't think this desire is wrong. In fact, I think it's in our nature. Play building blocks with any toddler and they will default to building as tall as they can as quickly as they can. If you want to be a witness to a tantrum, stay long enough to see their haphazardly constructed tower come crashing down.

We tend to throw tantrums too when the plans we've built don't meet our expectations.

In order to manage our expectations (and our tantrums) we need to understand the bigger picture of organizational life and the essential building blocks that support the health of our organization and our vision.

THE BUILDING BLOCKS

The life cycle of an organization is often depicted as a bell curve. We all aspire to go "up and to the right" as quickly as possible and do everything within our power to resist the backside of the life cycle, which depicts decline and ultimately death.

As a certified Scale Architect of Predictable Success[7] working with organizations on their strategies for growth, I repeatedly see two key areas that are often overlooked in the pursuit of growth. These two key things are foundational for organizational growth to occur.

1. Purpose
2. Culture

These are the foundational steps that support growth up and to the right. I picture it as a set of stairsteps undergirding the curve. Each one of these steps is a key facet of organizational development that we must attend to. If the first two steps of purpose and culture are given appropriate attention, the third step of strategy becomes a more natural overflow of our effort rather than an elusive target we can't hit.

The following graphic gives us a visual of the importance of these two steps that precede strategy. While strategy is important, a consistent focus on purpose—why we do what we do—coupled with a commitment to our people is essential for us to build the strategy on.

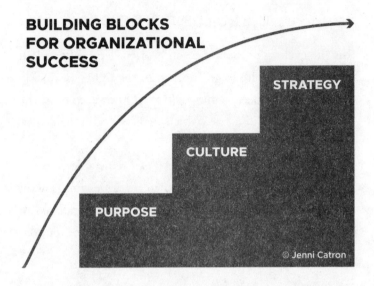

BUILDING BLOCKS
FOR ORGANIZATIONAL
SUCCESS

STRATEGY

CULTURE

PURPOSE

© Jenni Catron

3 CRITICAL CONSIDERATIONS

Let's look more closely at the relationship between these building blocks.

Without a keen sense of purpose, you will get crushed under the weight of responsibility as you scale up.

Most organizations start with a strong sense of purpose. You painstakingly craft your mission and vision. This is the only thing you have at the beginning, so you do the initial work to define it. This step is mostly below the surface. It's foundational. It is the biggest step and shoulders the most weight. It's the "why" behind everything you do.

The problem emerges as the organization grows. Demands of customers compromise your clarity of vision.

New staff members bring new ideas. Opportunities emerge that sound like a good idea, and before you realize it you lack clarity of purpose.

If your culture is not healthy, your strategy is irrelevant.
You may have heard the quote, "Culture eats strategy for breakfast." We even subscribe to axioms such as "People are our greatest asset."

We often give lip service to the importance of culture, but in the pursuit of organizational growth we focus our efforts on strategic plans, setting audacious goals, and implementing the systems and structures to support them. The busyness of these efforts often causes us to neglect the development of our teams and creating environments in which the very people we need to accomplish our vision can thrive.

The second step, culture, is the heart of the Lead-Culture Framework. It starts with our personal growth as a leader and extends to how we cultivate the development of our team. This step builds upon purpose in that you're helping a team of people personally and collectively act in congruence with the purpose of the organization.

Strategy only succeeds when it's aligned with purpose and culture.
It's not that strategy isn't important. It is. We need to know how we're going to accomplish our mission and vision, but this is often where I see leaders spend disproportionate amounts of time and energy. Eager to identify outcomes

and accomplish audacious goals, we quickly pursue the strategies that will make those goals possible, only to have spent significant budget to build a strategic plan that sits in a binder on a shelf.

---

*Strategy only succeeds when it's
aligned with purpose and culture.*

Leaders often call me when their repeated attempts at strategy are not resulting in growth. Their eye is on the top of the bell curve—that pinnacle of growth (however growth is defined for your organization). Unfortunately, I've heard story after story of leaders who have invested in strategic planning year after year with only unmet goals and frustration to show for it.

Where culture and strategy collide is where we see extraordinary outcomes, but we must give disproportionate time to culture development in order for strategy to be successful.

The weight of success will be crushing if we are not attending to our culture. If you trace the trajectory of an organization that has imploded, I'm confident you'll find a compromised culture beneath the rubble.

STEWARDSHIP OF PEOPLE

I was recently speaking at a conference and asked the attendees the following questions:

"How many of you have spent time, maybe even hired someone, to help you write your mission and vision statements for your organization?"

Nearly all the hands in the room went up. Then I asked, "How many of you have a written strategic plan?" Again, nearly every hand in the room went up.

Finally, I asked, "How many of you have a plan for your team culture?"

This time only a few hands went up. I wasn't surprised. In fact, as I referenced in the introduction, research tells us that while 90 percent of leaders believe that an employee engagement plan will help them achieve their mission, only 25 percent of them actually have a plan.

Why is it we fail to give the time and attention to arguably the greatest resource we have—our people?

Another way to think about culture is the stewardship of people in pursuit of a purpose. As a leader you are simultaneously juggling these two mandates: 1) to accomplish the purpose of your organization, and 2) to build and retain a great staff who make that purpose possible.

We live in an era of organizational leadership where employees have greater expectations of their work culture. They have more flexibility and more options than they've ever had. Work and life collide like never before and employees want to be a part of a culture that reflects the values they hold and connects them with work that has purpose and meaning. They are less fearful to change jobs and will prioritize seeking out work that provides fulfillment and purpose.

When we're intentional about designing and building our culture, great team members will clamor to be a part of it, and more importantly they'll want to remain a part of it. This dynamic creates a unique opportunity for leaders to build cultures in which purpose is clear and team members can find meaning in their contribution.

As leaders who are shaping the culture of our teams, it's our responsibility to bring clarity to who we are and how we work to achieve our mission. Whether it's two people or two thousand, you have the opportunity, privilege, and responsibility to be intentional in leading culture.

Culture isn't just a nice idea that you'll get to if you have time. It's the very linchpin that ties your purpose and strategy together. You can't achieve your purpose without a team of people to make it happen.

FROM CAUGHT TO TAUGHT

Have you ever watched five-year-olds play soccer? If you're remotely competitive, this experience is absolutely maddening. A mob of small children huddle around the ball and move in a big blob up and down the field. There is no strategy. No differentiation in responsibilities. They collectively chase the ball together and hope to score a goal here or there.

This is how many of us approach our culture. When your team is small, you essentially do everything together. While you might be very strategic in the key areas of your business, you treat culture like an amorphous blob of soccer-playing five-year-olds. Simply by chance and proximity you score a few culture wins, and you keep blissfully enjoying the game.

For a small team, in the early days, culture is mostly caught. You're with each other all the time and sheer proximity enables you to understand "this is who we are and how we work together." You don't have stated values because they are understood. You know "how we do things here."

This is all well and good until growth makes it impossible to sustain. Before long you find yourself saying things like, "That's not how we do things here." What used to be so clear is suddenly chaotic and frustrating. You feel like you're losing control, and you find yourself becoming the bottleneck for all decision-making.

CULTURE AS A SYSTEM

We hold our breath and cross our fingers when our team is thriving. We just hope beyond hope it will stay that way but we're not sure how we got there and we're afraid one wrong move could topple it all. We're often unsure of what makes it go well and what makes it go poorly.

Add to that myriad responsibilities we're juggling to keep the organization moving, and culture gets relegated to the back burner. It's not on fire so hopefully it will all be okay. But as the familiar adage goes, "hope is not a strategy."

That's the problem I see too many leaders making— hoping that their culture will be okay or work itself out. If we sniff a few problems, we delegate it to HR and hope it gets better soon. But it doesn't go away. Culture exists whether you acknowledge it or not and it doesn't get better on its own.

This is when culture must move from caught to taught. The organic nature of your culture has met its end and without an intentional commitment to build a plan to define and embed your culture, the frustrations you're feeling will only get worse.

Healthy, sustainable, scalable culture needs leadership and it needs a system. Just like every other organizational initiative, great culture needs a plan. You're not going to accidentally arrive at your desired destination. The longer you ignore it, the more work you'll have ahead of you. You have to define it to achieve it.

I want to acknowledge here that talking about creating a system for culture may feel counterintuitive. Culture is about people and, therefore, to systematize it raises concerns that you'll lose the heart, connection, and camaraderie that have been the best of your culture so far. I want to assure you that the clearer you get about your culture and the system you've built to support it, the more connected and engaged your team members will feel.

THE RELATIONSHIP BETWEEN
LEADERSHIP AND CULTURE

I hear the frustration from leaders nearly daily that the responsibility of building and leading a team caught them off guard. Of course they want a team that is aligned and working effectively together. Of course they want a culture that attracts and retains the best talent. But where is the manual for building that? When does the whirlwind of organizational life slow down enough to provide the luxury of learning these skills that are so essential and yet apparently not so important that we prioritize the time to train for them?

That's the problem with leadership—for many, leadership tends to sneak up on you. One day you're grinding it out, trying to simply succeed at the role you've been given, and the next you look up and you're responsible for a team of people.

As a result, we're left with a chasm between the leaders who intuitively understand culture and prioritize people development and those who don't. Or worse, we have well-intentioned champions of culture who talk a big culture game and have all the external appearances of a great culture while internal dialogue of team members speaks more of a toxic environment. Perhaps one of the more recent examples is of Adam Neumann and the infamous rise and fall of his coworking company, WeWork, which one writer described as "a wild ride in Unicornland."[8] WeWork boasted free meals, an onsite barista, posh office spaces, and outrageous staff retreats while behind the scenes employees shared concerns of cultlike behaviors, toxic positivity, extravagant spending, operational chaos, and skepticism of leadership decisions.

Great culture is built with intuitive leadership and an intentional plan, both of which can be learned, and this book is designed to equip you with the leadership insights and an actionable plan to build an extraordinary culture.

If you're one of those leaders who intuitively gets the value of culture, I suspect you've picked up this book because a) you want to keep learning and growing (yay, you!), or b) something in your culture has gone awry and you're struggling to diagnose why. Since you didn't have a plan for building the culture you have, it's difficult to diagnose when it goes wrong. You can learn the plan part of the equation, which is going to help you build an even stronger culture.

And as for that fraction of narcissistic leaders who create the appearance of great culture when everyone around them whispers the reality, I'm confident they aren't reading this book because their culture will have completely imploded before they realized something was wrong.

Personally, I didn't know how to build culture and, frankly, building a great team culture was nowhere on my radar when I began to take on greater leadership responsibility. Perhaps like you, leadership and culture snuck up on me. I didn't understand the value and I didn't prioritize it. Fortunately, I was part of an organization that did and I got a jump start on my understanding of the essential skills to lead well.

YOU ARE THE KEY TO YOUR CULTURE

Before we can dig into the nuts and bolts of how to build a great team, let me establish that what *you* believe as the leader matters. In order to build an extraordinary team culture that great people are clamoring to be a part of, you need to know what you believe about leadership and specifically about your leadership in creating team culture.

Here's what won't work:

- You won't build a great team culture if you're doing it only because someone told you to do it.
- You won't build a great team culture if you're doing it because it seems to be the organizational focus du jour, aka all the cool leaders are doing it.
- You won't build a great team culture if you're doing it for selfish reasons, perhaps to make yourself look better or solely to achieve all your goals.

The reality of building great teams is that they take work. They take perseverance. They take patience. They take a willingness to adjust your pace, your style, and your preferences for the greater good of the team.

For this book to lead to change in your team and organization, it has to start with you. You must embrace a perspective shift that prioritizes the good of the team over your goals and ambitions. It's not that you can't have goals and ambitions. In fact, as you'll learn a bit later, a key element of great teams is that they have clear, shared goals. But first, you need to understand how to lead you.

One of my notorious sayings is, "You must lead yourself well to lead others better." Self-leadership is the starting point of all leadership. If you want to lead your team to a new outcome—to a new culture—it must start with you.

Remember how I told you I like to move fast? Nothing about building an extraordinary team is fast. In fact, research tells us that substantially changing your organization or team culture can be a three-to-five-year process. Yep, *not* fast!

> ***Self-leadership is the starting point of all leadership.***

This commitment of time and energy is why we're often unwilling to do the real work necessary to build a strong foundation for team culture. We're going to have to slow down. We're going to have to take time and engage the process. And for most leaders I know, the idea of a multi-year commitment to see the change they want feels so over-whelming they go back to business as usual.

This is why many of our organizations are fraught with a revolving door of employees. We no sooner fill a position than another one opens up. It's HR Whac-A-Mole. Not only are we dealing with the frustration of recruiting, inter-viewing, onboarding, training, etc., that is required every time a team member transitions, but the hard and soft costs to our organization are exponential. Research tells us that it can cost as much as two to three times the annual salary of the position when a transition occurs. And that's just the hard costs. It's difficult to put a price tag on the emotional toll on you, your HR team, and other staff that are having to compensate in time and energy for the open role.

Do you really want to continue to do business as usual, losing valuable time and energy with staff that are only partially engaged or are quick to move on to the next "great opportunity"?

What if you could create a culture where you experience:

- an engaged and energized team who enjoy working together
- a team where infighting and politicking are rare or unheard of and definitely not tolerated
- a team where great people stay, and turnover is low
- a team that shares the same values and are committed to one another
- a team that is highly productive
- a team that is aligned to the mission, vision, and values across all departments

This is not just "Jenni's magical dreams of great teams"; this is possible. I've seen it. I've experienced it. I've built these kinds of teams. Better yet, I've led hundreds of other leaders to embrace these principles and build extraordinary teams too. Now I'm committed to helping you!

The LeadCulture Framework:
Your Culture Operating System

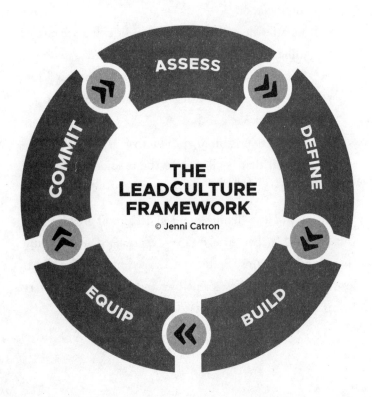

PHASE 1

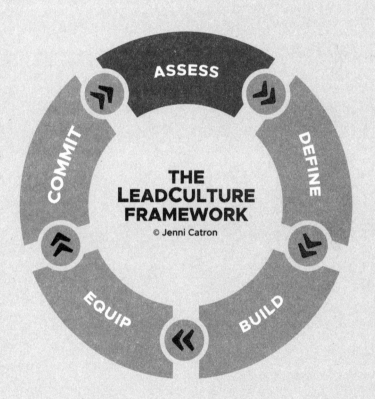

2

Getting Clear on
Your Culture

"Respect is the currency of great cultures."
—Matthew Kelly[9]

I don't know what's wrong, but we need help." Those were the first words out of Steve's mouth when we connected.

Steve is the founder of an influential nonprofit organization throughout the Greater Chicago area with impact around the globe. I had worked with Steve and his team on and off for over seven years, so I was very familiar with their work and with the culture of the team.

Steve's a great leader with a great team but something was off, and he knew he needed help diagnosing it. They had shifted some strategies that resulted in sizable changes throughout the organization and his team was feeling the pressure. Steve is a leader I know well. He's trustworthy. He's deeply committed to the mission of the organization. He loves his team, and he sincerely wants everyone to thrive. And yet they weren't.

Steve needed help assessing what exactly was going on in their culture.

GET HONEST

You can't map the route to your destination if you don't know where you are.

Your dream as a leader is to have a team of people on a mission with you. There is nothing better than winning with great people. But you wake up every day worrying about the hard conversation you need to have, the challenging personality that keeps testing your patience, or the wonderfully sweet person who is grossly incompetent.

You have a vague idea of what a great culture looks like, but you are at a loss for how to get there.

The starting point for building an extraordinary culture is assessing where you currently are. Good, bad, or unfortunate, you need to get honest about the reality of your culture. The difficult thing for most leaders to understand is that your culture is rarely as good as you think it is. Culture always feels the best at the top of the organization. The primary reason for this is that you hold more influence on your experience in the organization. If you don't like something, you have the agency to change it.

Too often leaders are dismissive of cultural undercurrents because they don't feel the effects of them. The best thing you can do for you and your team is to be willing to get honest about what's true.

As you make a commitment to assess your culture, you will find some things that pleasantly surprise you and uncover other things that gravely disappoint you. This is where I beg you to lead yourself well. Be incredibly self-aware of your reactions and responses. Put on your "curiosity hat" and develop a sincere desire to understand what is true about your culture today.

An honest starting point is essential and I'm going to give you the tools to make a healthy evaluation of the state of your culture.

Too often leaders are dismissive of cultural undercurrents because they don't feel the effects of them.

With Steve's team, I started my work by interviewing various team members to get their perspective and insights. What I quickly discovered were the typical culture-busting behaviors that plague many teams—confusion, chaos, suspicion, competition, and mistrust. As I talked to each team member, they still expressed hope, they wanted to believe the best overall, but their day-to-day interactions were tense, and that tension was only growing. It was clear that without some course correction, the connection and camaraderie that used to be a hallmark of this team would be lost.

To begin our work, we needed clarity.

CULTURE HIERARCHY OF NEEDS

You may remember learning in psychology class about Maslow's Hierarchy of Needs.

"Maslow's hierarchy of needs is a motivational theory in psychology comprising a five-tier model of human needs, often depicted as hierarchical levels within a pyramid. . . .

"From the bottom of the hierarchy upwards, the needs are: physiological [food and clothing], safety, love and belonging, esteem and self-actualization." Maslow's belief was that "needs lower down in the hierarchy must be satisfied before individuals can attend to needs higher up."[10]

CULTURE HIERARCHY OF NEEDS

PERSONAL FULFILLMENT

CONNECTION

PSYCHOLOGICAL SAFETY

ORGANIZATIONAL CLARITY

BASIC NEEDS

© Jenni Catron

Similar to Maslow's hierarchy, there is a hierarchy of employee needs that impact the culture of your team. Let's call it the Culture Hierarchy of Needs.

Like Maslow's hierarchy, there are five needs that impact a team member's ability to grow with your organization and positively contribute to the health of your culture. To truly build an extraordinary culture, attending to these five needs is essential.

THE 5 LEVELS OF THE HIERARCHY

Basic Needs

The first level of the hierarchy is about an employee's basic needs to succeed in the organization. Every new employee is reduced to baseline needs when they take a new job or assume a new role. There are two key categories of needs: what they need to do their work and why they need to do it. Essentially, they need to be equipped with the practical tools and information for their role and they need to understand the purpose for it.

This level of the hierarchy is about equipping employees with the basic tools they need to know how to effectively contribute to the organization. This includes:

- Clarity of purpose (the organization's mission and vision)
- Fair compensation
- Onboarding to culture and systems
- Practical tools for their role
- Training and development

Organizational Clarity

The second level of the hierarchy, organizational clarity, is arguably the most critical level of the culture hierarchy. This level of the hierarchy is the single greatest differentiator between extraordinary teams and mediocre teams.

Organizational clarity means I understand what is expected of me, I have clarity of my place in the organization, and my role and responsibilities are clear. This stage answers the questions "Who are we?" and "How do we work together to achieve our mission?" When leaders explain these core essentials, they provide organizational clarity, and team members can be secure in their role and their place on the team.

This level of the hierarchy involves providing:

- Clarity for shared goals
- Clarity of organizational structure
- Clarity for defined roles and responsibilities
- Clarity of the values and behaviors that define success for the team

Psychological Safety

Psychological safety is about employees feeling emotionally secure when they are at work. It's really a fancy phrase for trust. Employees will feel empowered when they are part of an environment where they feel trusted and respected. Psychological safety gives team members the confidence to contribute wholeheartedly.

Organizational psychologist Adam Grant explains it this way: "Psychological safety is not a matter of relaxing standards, making people comfortable, being nice and agreeable, or giving unconditional praise. It's fostering a climate of respect, trust, and openness in which people can raise concerns and suggestions without fear of reprisal."[11]

It builds upon the first two needs in that if I have the tools I need to do my job and I've been provided clarity for what to do and how to do it, I am prepared to better engage with my team. In order to find synergy and alignment, team members need to build trust and respect for one another, be self-aware and others-aware, and feel like they can actively bring their best work.

Connection

One of our great needs as humans is belonging. We are wired for community. We're designed to do life with others. It's the functional definition of the word *team*—two or more people working together to achieve a goal.

Research tells us that employees don't quit jobs, they quit people.[12] If employees have their basic needs met (level 1), they have clarity in their work (level 2), and they feel comfortable to actively contribute (level 3), they will naturally build connections with their coworkers. When we're addressing this need, team members want to be together.

As leaders, we foster this and protect this need of culture by ensuring that we have organizational rhythms that allow for connection and that we create a culture of mutual commitment and accountability. It's important that we don't create false harmony or toxic positivity, but that we lean into the principles of healthy relationships where candor, honesty, and integrity drive our interactions with one another. The values we defined in level two must be consistently lived for level four to be realized.

Personal Fulfillment

This final level is an outcome. You can't force anyone to find personal fulfillment in their work, but you can create an environment that fosters it by attending to the first four needs and thereby setting the stage for this one to be achieved as well.

When team members are personally fulfilled, they are fully utilizing their gifts with a team that they love, doing work that is fulfilling. The best part of this is that when team members are operating at this level, they are actively reproducing this in others. They notice other team members at different levels and are personally invested in helping everyone on the team move through the hierarchy of needs.

When an organization's culture achieves the Culture Hierarchy of Needs, employees are less likely to be among the 85 percent[13] considering a job change because they have found purpose and meaning in their work.

The hierarchy provides a roadmap for assessing your organizational culture. Understanding these fundamental needs and being purposeful to meet them will give you the clarity you need to achieve the culture you want. As we work through the assessment phase, we'll use the hierarchy as our guide.

THE RELATIONSHIP BETWEEN CLARITY AND TRUST

Think for a moment about one of the best work experiences you've been a part of. I bet I can predict what you experienced:

- You worked for a leader you admired and respected.
- You had coworkers who were also friends.
- You enjoyed the organization because you felt like the work you were doing had purpose and meaning.
- You were passionate about your role because you understood your responsibilities and what was expected of you.
- You were excited about the mission of the organization.

If I had to boil all those things down to one word, I'd say that word is *trust*. You trusted your leader. You trusted your coworkers. You trusted the mission of the organization. You trusted what was expected of you.

So now, my question is, Why? Why did you have that trust? What created that level of trust?

Trust is the foundation of teams. Trust is the currency of healthy working relationships.

Most of us absolutely believe trust is key. We're not arguing with the premise, but we find ourselves perplexed with what to do when trust is lacking. Trust falls and team bonding activities generally invoke eye rolls. We know it's more than that.

We often think, *Maybe the team needs more time together* or, *We need to focus on relationships and connection.* And yes, those things are a good start—after all, it's difficult to build trust without relationships.

But as I've worked with hundreds of teams and analyzed cultures of all sizes, I've found that there are some relatively simple things we can do as leaders to build trust in our organization that will lead to a stronger and healthier culture.

In Steve's case, the question that was haunting him was: What caused a team that was thriving to seemingly overnight find themselves struggling? I identified that Steve's team had lost two things: clarity and trust. A lack of clarity always leads to a lack of trust.

Trust may be one of the most problematic words for leaders and teams. We know what it feels like to trust and be trusted but we often struggle to know what builds it or erodes it.

In Patrick Lencioni's *The Five Dysfunctions of a Team* he lists "absence of trust" as the first dysfunction that derails teams. That's probably not shocking to you. The question most of us wrestle with is, How exactly do we build trust, especially within an organization? Many leaders think they have this figured out.

In short: relationships. When you're launching something new and building a new team, you as the leader are personally recruiting each person. You're tapping friends and former coworkers on the shoulder and you're building a team based upon relationships. Even if you hire a friend of a friend, you quickly get to know that new person, a relationship is formed, and trust is built.

In small teams, relationship equals trust.

This works for a while until the growth of the organization eclipses your ability to give time and proximity to every team member. A growing organization means the staff is growing, which means suddenly the things that relationships need to flourish—time and proximity—are getting stretched thin. Lack of time and lack of proximity in which to build relationships results in eroding trust, or in some cases never developing it. The new employee who met the senior leader in one staff meeting a few months ago never had the privilege of proximity that fuels relationships that spark trust.

A lack of clarity always leads to a lack of trust.

When teams are expecting relationships alone to build trust, leaders are going to be digging through an avalanche of unmet expectations.

For the first part of my career, I worked on small teams of five to twenty-five people. Trust was high because relationships were how we operated. It wasn't until I was dropped into a 100-plus-person team that I realized my relationship-building skills alone weren't enough. In fact, in the team that I joined, there was skepticism of my desire to get to know others. They didn't want relationship with me as much as they wanted leadership from me.

My personal experiences coupled with the learnings from working with hundreds of organizations on their culture have helped me realize that trust in an organizational setting is built through competence. While our dazzling personalities might pull us through when the team is small and time together covers a multitude of competency deficiencies, a larger team and a more mature organization needs the confidence of your competence to trust your leadership.

The competence that I'm talking about here has to do with the organizational clarity you are providing the team and the disciplines that guide the behavior of the team. What I've found repeatedly is that if we desire a culture where staff feel personally fulfilled (top of the hierarchy) and are enjoying connection and belonging (level 4) in an environment where they can confidently engage (level 3), we as leaders must first provide the clarity and the disciplines that help ensure team members of what it takes to succeed.

In his book *Effortless*, Greg McKeown defines low-trust versus high-trust in this way:

> A low-trust structure is one where expectations are unclear, where goals are incompatible or at odds, where people don't know who is doing what, where the rules are ambiguous and nobody knows what the standards for success are, and where the priorities are unclear and the incentives misaligned.
>
> A high-trust structure is one where expectations are clear. Goals are shared, roles are clearly delineated, the rules and standards are articulated, and the right

results are prioritized, incentivized, and rewarded—consistently, not just sometimes.[14]

This is why organizational clarity precedes psychological safety on the Culture Hierarchy of Needs. Funny enough, this still comes down to relationship but in a slightly different way. Organizational leaders have a responsibility to provide the structure and the clarity that equips team members to know how to succeed. Our part of the relationship in a healthy organizational structure is to provide what the employees need.

Think about it this way: If you didn't consistently provide a home, food, and clothing for your family, how much would they trust you? They might genuinely love you because of the personal relationship you have, but if every day they wondered where they would sleep or what they would eat, they probably wouldn't have a lot of trust in your ability to provide for them.

Similarly, trust with our team members relies on our ability to provide what they need to successfully contribute in their role. Everything we do in the first two levels of the hierarchy is building or eroding trust.

The LeadCulture Framework will guide you to take a closer look at the contributing elements to culture at each of these levels and equip you to take action that builds trust with your team.

3

Getting Feedback

"A brave leader is someone who says I see
you. I hear you. I don't have all the answers,
but I'm going to keep listening and asking
questions."

—Brené Brown[15]

Jenni, I'm nervous. I love my team. I thought they were
okay, but now I'm wondering if there was more going
on than I was aware of. I'm anxious about what they will
share," Steve vulnerably confided as I was outlining the first
phase of our work.

I appreciated his honesty. He wasn't being dismissive
and just going through the motions. He genuinely cared
about his team and was willing to make himself uncomfortable to get an honest assessment of the state of their culture.

WHAT'S TRUE?

As much as you want to know what is true about your current culture, it's a very vulnerable question for most leaders to ask. In many ways it feels like an indictment on your leadership and it's incredibly discouraging to discover that your employees are not as engaged as you would hope.

This part of the process is crucial to building the healthy culture you aspire to. As a leader, you must demonstrate a sincere desire to understand what's true in your culture. This requires you to lead with emotional intelligence. You need to be self-aware of your fears, frustrations, and insecurities and conscious of how those feelings are showing up to the team. If they sense that you're not committed to getting to the truth, they will hold back. It's equally as vulnerable for the team to give honest feedback about what they are experiencing in the organization.

Before I make it sound too ominous, there are also some wonderful things you'll discover about your culture. Both will exist. There is no perfect culture. There is no perfect team. We're a bunch of messy humans aiming to do good work together and there will be both beauty and chaos in this work. Your job is to elevate the beauty and reduce the chaos. You can't do that without an honest assessment of what's true now.

Assessing your current culture requires a combination of anonymous surveying of the entire team as well as focus group conversations using the hierarchy of needs as your framework for assessment.

SURVEYS

To begin the assessment phase of our work, I met with Steve and his leadership team to craft a customized survey that would be sent to all of their nearly one hundred staff members. Part 1 of the survey included the standard Lead-Culture questions framed around the Culture Hierarchy of Needs, and Part 2 was a set of questions based upon their existing staff values. My team and I worked closely with Steve to ensure good communication of the process as well as to encourage the team to share honestly and openly. Not surprisingly, we had to assure the team that their answers were truly anonymous. A few team members expressed concern over how their honesty would be received by senior leadership. This hinted at a lack of psychological safety in the culture that we were mindful to take note of.

Pros and Cons of Surveys

In the assessment phase of the LeadCulture Framework, you are creating the map of your cultural landscape. Each tool in the assessment process is providing a bit more detail to help you understand the terrain. You're on an expedition to find the best of your culture, but you're also going to discover some pitfalls and some obstacles along the way. Both offer insight and clues to help you get to your desired destination.

An employee engagement survey is one of the tools you'll use in this phase. Surveys are a very common tool for getting feedback about your organizational culture. The resources are endless, and the opinions are plentiful about the use of surveys for gauging the health of your team. At their best, surveys are a tool to help you acquire valuable feedback from your entire team. However, they are not perfect. Let's look at some of their pros and cons.

The pros of surveys:
- Provide an opportunity for every team member to give feedback
- Give you comprehensive feedback from throughout the organization, not just the loudest voices
- Provide data to inform further discussion and discovery

The cons of surveys:
- If employees are fearful of how leadership will respond, they may not be fully honest
- Often result in more questions than answers
- Timing may influence results—can be influenced by when they were taken (i.e., if it's a busy or stressful season, that is likely to be disproportionately reflected in the results)
- Interpretation can be subjective

Why Benchmarking Against Others Is a Poor Evaluation

A common practice for many survey tools is to provide benchmarking against other organizations in your industry. I understand the desire to do this. We're conditioned to want to know how we measure up to our peers. I hold a contrarian view on this practice because I've seen it become a vanity metric that often ends up being more detrimental to your culture. By seeking to be a top organization among your peers, the goal becomes the designation rather than truly building a healthy culture. In some organizations, this has manifested in pressure on team members to answer the survey in such a way that they hit their goal of being a top organization rather than answering the survey truthfully. The pursuit of the status becomes the goal rather than the pursuit of being a healthy team.

My conviction is that every organization needs to benchmark against themselves by creating a survey that evaluates two key things:

1. The core needs of every team member as described in the Culture Hierarchy of Needs
2. The customized questions that are designed to assess how effectively you're reflecting the culture you aspire to (often based upon your values)

By focusing on evaluating what you've defined as a healthy culture for your team, you're getting better feedback on how you're doing in measuring up to your standard of success, not the standards set by others. After all, every culture is unique. How your team works together to achieve your mission is going to be different from another organization, even a competitor or peer, and therefore what you measure must be different. When you focus on evaluating your unique culture and you create a rhythm of evaluating this consistently, you then can benchmark against yourself.

You'll be able to see your progress from year to year on the things that uniquely define your culture.

I don't care how you stack up to other organizations. I care how you stack up against who you've said you want to be. In Phase 2 of the framework, I'll help you define this.

Surveying Best Practices

1. Choose a survey tool that assesses what is most important to you and commit to using this tool. Changing survey tools each year will not allow for the benchmarking against yourself that ultimately helps you consistently assess the health of your culture.

2. Establish a regular rhythm of surveying (I recommend once a year) so that you can begin to see movement toward your desired culture.

3. Engage a third-party organization to conduct the survey and compile results. This gives your team confidence that their answers are truly anonymous and increases trust in the process. (See page 274 for an overview of the LeadCulture survey.)

FOCUS GROUPS

With survey data in hand, it was time to facilitate conversations with other members of Steve's team who could bring more color and perspective to what the data was saying. To help me get a clear understanding of the challenges the team was facing, I needed to hear directly from more team members. I wanted to be able to ask them questions and observe their responses. I needed to hear their observations and interpretations.

Focus group discussions will reveal things that can't fully be captured in a survey. The legends and language of your culture are important aspects for assessing your culture, and you need to create environments for them to be drawn out.

BUILD A CULTURE TEAM

Because culture work is an ongoing process and not an episodic event, choosing a Culture Champion and a Culture Team is an important part of setting your work up for success.

Your Culture Champion could be you or it may be another senior leader who can be the ongoing champion of your culture. This individual should be someone who is passionate about this work and who has been given this responsibility as part of their job profile. This is not a short-term project. This is an ongoing commitment, and it needs to be given appropriate priority. Your Culture Champion needs to wake up every day thinking about the health of your team.

Your Culture Champion ideally should be a part of the executive team so that they have a voice and influence with the organization's most senior leaders and are at the table for key decisions that may impact culture. Depending on the size of your organization, this may be a dedicated role like a Chief Culture Officer or a Director of People and Culture or it may be combined with other job responsibilities.

The Culture Team's mandate is to represent the entire staff with the goal of surfacing an honest assessment of the culture and then to define the preferred future. Initially, your Culture Team will have a project-based commission. They will partner with your Culture Champion to work through the five phases of the LeadCulture Framework. Usually, this process will take six to twelve months depending on the pacing of the work and significance of the change you need to make. After their initial project, you may decide to extend this team's responsibilities, swap out some team members, or leave your Culture Champion to assemble special project teams as needed. The plan you outline in Phase 3 will influence how you use your Culture Team moving forward.

How to Choose Your Culture Team

Selection for this team is not based on role or hierarchy, but rather should be a group of team members who are committed to partnering with you on this work.

- Select eight to ten engaged staff members who reflect the best of your culture and are committed to the mission.
- Choose staff who are leaders from all levels of the organization and have influence with their peers

so that every staff member feels represented by the group.

- Invite team members who aren't always the primary decision makers because we don't want culture to feel like it's being directed from the top down.
- Select staff members who bring different personalities and perspectives to the conversation.
- Choose team members who reflect diversity in age, stage of life, race, ethnicity, gender, tenure on staff, etc.

A note of caution: Resist selecting the people who you most frequently go to for special projects. If employees perceive that you've chosen your "favorites" for this team, the team will lose credibility before it has even started.

Steve quickly identified his Culture Champion—in fact he had recently promoted one of his most trusted team members, Elizabeth, to Director of Culture and Staff Development. Elizabeth was deeply committed to building a great culture, but she wasn't sure where to start. The Lead-Culture Framework and my coaching were about to give her the support she needed.

Now we needed to build their Culture Team, and this is where it got more interesting. I asked Steve and Elizabeth to each compile a list of eight people they thought should be on the team. When we met to review their lists, they both expressed how hard it was to narrow their choices. They struggled to exclude some of the other senior leaders, and they feared not inviting people who would expect to be selected. What I discovered is that before we had even started the work, some of the more troublesome members of their culture were some of the loudest voices in their heads as they made their selections. After some rigorous discussion and some hard decisions, Steve and Elizabeth finally selected the eight individuals they would invite to join them as part of the Culture Team.

Culture Team Commitments

The work of the Culture Team is critical to the success of your culture change. Your Culture Team in a sense becomes an incubator for living into the preferred future of your entire culture. The values, beliefs, and behaviors you hope to be true of your entire team will be forged here first. This is why the selection of this team is critical.

Your Culture Team immediately becomes an ambassador for the work you've committed to, so it's essential they begin to operate in a way that breaks old habits and begins to reflect the future for your entire staff.

To accomplish this, the Culture Team must make the following commitments:

To think on behalf of the entire organization and all staff members.
The Culture Team must embrace what Les McKeown, in his book *The Synergist*, calls "the enterprise commitment." "When working in a team or a group environment . . . to place the interests of the enterprise above their personal

interests."[16] They need to embrace the responsibility of leadership and engage the work with a comprehensive view of what is good for the entire organization.

To be aware of their bias or preferences.
I've already referenced emotional intelligence and specifically self-awareness several times and it cannot be overstated here. Every team member will need to be exceptionally self-aware as they engage this work. They will need to bring a level of maturity to the conversations that leads to real change for the organization; otherwise they'll continue to stay stuck in the same patterns and behaviors that you're currently not satisfied with.

To set ground rules for how they'll engage.
As a group, the Culture Team will need to agree upon a set of values and behaviors for their engagement in the Lead-Culture Framework. This exercise is a bit of foreshadowing of the work they'll do for the entire organization. They will need to define values that reflect how they will contribute effectively in this work. For example, Culture Teams will commonly choose the value statement "we commit to candor." They understand that unless they are willing to be brutally (but graciously) honest with one another, they will not be able to lead the change they hope to see.

Culture Team Priorities

With your team assembled you're ready to get to work. In the assessment phase, the Culture Team has four priorities:

1. To review the data from the survey
2. To engage in rigorous conversations about what's true of the culture right now
3. To mine for and commit to honest evaluation
4. To determine what additional assessment work is needed

Let's look at each of these a bit closer.

Review the Data

Your culture survey holds important information both explicitly and implicitly. Meaning, you'll have some clear metrics, such as, only 25 percent of the team trust the senior leadership, but then as you read the comment section you may notice statements that seem to contradict that. For Steve's organization we discovered the team respected the executive team as individuals but lacked respect for their decision-making. A subtlety in their comments gave us more insight into that data point.

While I believe data is very powerful, it also can be limiting. Data becomes most helpful when it equips you to ask better questions. As you review and reflect on the data, let it spark questions that you discuss as a Culture Team.

Rigorous Conversations

At one point in our discussion, the room got awkward and quiet. I had just asked the team why they thought trust was lacking with their senior leaders. Admittedly, this is a hard question to answer, but it was necessary, and I knew they had opinions. Letting them escape the discomfort was ultimately not going to help them in the long run, so I let us all sit in the uncomfortable silence.

Before long Alli bravely spoke up: "I'm going to do my best to say this in an honoring way . . . because I don't mean any disrespect . . . but I think the reason that it's sometimes difficult for us to trust our senior leaders is because they don't always communicate very clearly about the decisions they make. I'm not even sure we disagree with the decisions. It's just that they seem haphazard. And because they don't involve us in the process, they don't understand the impact decisions have on other team members."

Immediately, the room heaved a sigh of relief and other team members expanded upon what Alli had shared. Their commitment to rigorous conversation, even when it was uncomfortable, resulted in a huge point of awareness for their culture.

After listening to the team share for several minutes, Steve eventually chimed in: "Thank you all for being willing to share that. I'm guessing that it wasn't easy, and it's a little hard to hear, but this is really helpful. I had no idea the turbulence some of our decisions were creating. I see how important it is for us as a leadership team to be more intentional in clearly communicating decisions. If this is the only thing that comes from this work, it will be a game changer for our culture!"

The best results of your culture work will come from a team that is committed to rigorous conversation. You'll want to push for differing opinions and honest debate. Depending on your existing culture, this will likely be very uncomfortable for some members of the team. This is when you remind everyone of the commitments you made as a team and harken back to the values you set for how you would operate together.

Here are some common discussion starters:

- What is right, wrong, confused, or missing in our current culture?[17]
- What do we look like at our best?
- If you could magically infuse all our employees with three qualities, what would they be?[18]
- What would someone new to our team say we value as an organization?
- What are we most proud of?
- What are we least proud of?
- What would we change about our team if we could just snap our fingers and make it happen?

Honest Evaluation

As you surface observations about your current culture, you'll have moments of deep pride and moments of disappointment. Everyone wants to be a part of a healthy culture and it can be easy to dismiss some of the observations both in the data and in the conversations as episodic. You'll be prone to make excuses and possibly even dismiss what was brought up. I want to encourage you to fight this tendency. The more willing you are to dig deeper and honestly evaluate what was uncovered, the greater chance you have to change your culture for the good.

What Else?

In many cases you'll walk away from these initial conversations with more questions than answers. That's not uncommon and it's okay. Curiosity is your friend in this process. Identify where you need more insight to help the team gain better understanding and then make a plan to get more information.

You might do this by:

- Creating a short (emphasis on *short*) follow-up survey (over-surveying can be detrimental to your culture so use this one sparingly).
- Conducting some focus group discussions with other staff members. One team I worked with hosted three brown bag lunch discussions for anyone on the staff who wanted to participate. They identified three core issues in their survey that they felt they needed more information about to help them devise a plan to address.
- Commissioning the Culture Team to have one-on-one conversations with other staff members as appropriate. One word of caution here: make sure these conversations stay at a fact-finding, problem-solving level and don't devolve into gossip or complaining. You want to ensure that the conversations around assessing your culture keep a

hopeful and honest tone. Not toxic positivity but also not negative or degrading.

CULTURE TEAM
ACTION PLAN

↳ Select and build your initial survey. Note that because you have not done the definition phase yet, you will not have the customized portion for this first survey. You'll add that for the next time you survey.

↳ Conduct your survey.

↳ Gather as a Culture Team to discuss, debate, and clarify the current state of your culture based upon the survey data.

CLARITY CHECK

	Yes	No
We have a Culture Champion.	☐	☐
Our Culture Champion is on the Executive Team.	☐	☐
We have selected our Culture Team.	☐	☐

	Yes	No
We have chosen our survey tool.	☐	☐
We have conducted an anonymous staffwide survey and reviewed the results.	☐	☐

If you checked **No** to any of the clarity check statements, I encourage you to spend more time completing those items before moving forward in the process.

PHASE 2

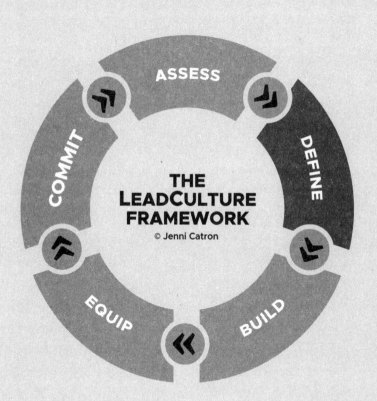

4

Clarifying Who You Are

"Culture is the vision, values, systems, language, expectations, behaviors, and beliefs that increase or decrease an organization's chances of accomplishing its strategy and fulfilling its mission, which in turn increases or decreases how much people enjoy coming to work."

—Matthew Kelly[19]

The assessment phase was very eye-opening for Steve and his team. Using the hierarchy of needs as their guide, they gained greater awareness of where the gaps were that were creating confusion and frustration for the entire staff. They identified their core issues and were now ready to move to the next phase: Define. One of their most interesting aha moments so far had been how the things that felt clear, especially to senior leaders like Steve, were not nearly as clear for many of the other team members. They were quickly understanding how much a lack of clarity erodes trust in the culture and they knew that this next phase would require them to be very intentional to bring more clarity to their culture.

WHAT ARE YOU AIMING FOR?

Most leaders have a vague idea of what a great culture looks like. They observe other teams in their best moments and are tempted to mimic their practices rather than do the work to uncover what is most unique about their own team.

Culture is clarity of who you are and how you work together to achieve your mission.

I've referenced my definition of culture a few times so far, but it's worth pausing to take a closer look at this definition.

Culture is clarity of who you are and how you work together to achieve your mission.

There are three key parts of this definition:

1. Who you are
2. How you work together
3. Your mission

These three keys will help you define the culture you aspire to.

YOUR MISSION

Let's start with the end in mind. Who you are and how you work together is ultimately to serve the purpose of achieving your mission. Your team would not exist if there wasn't a mission for you to accomplish. This isn't a social club. This is a team on a mission. In order to rally a team to achieve a mission, they need to know and understand what that mission is and then they need to know how to behave in a way that helps make that mission happen. Culture is clarity of who you are and how you work together *to achieve your mission.*

In simplest terms, your mission is a succinct, memorable phrase that communicates why you do what you do and typically includes who you're doing the work for. The power of a mission statement is that it is timeless. How you carry out your mission may change with your strategic planning, but your mission—your core *why*—will remain the same.

Qualities of a Great Mission Statement

It is clear and concise.
You want a mission statement that is ideally one phrase— even better if it's less than twenty words. Short and to the point. You don't need a bunch of fluffy words and phrases that look impressive but are impossible to remember. You want your team to grasp, own, and repeat that statement after hearing it just a couple of times.

Here are a few examples of clear and concise mission statements:

- 4Sight's mission statement: "To cultivate healthy leaders to lead thriving teams."
- REI: "To inspire, educate and outfit for a lifetime of outdoor adventure and stewardship."
- Etsy: "To keep human connection at the heart of commerce."
- LEGO: "To inspire and develop the builders of tomorrow."[20]

It paints of a picture of what you do and who it's for.
A good mission statement helps every team member remember what we do and for whom. When they feel lost in the mundane details, reconnecting with the mission statement helps provide the bigger picture for their work.

It is memorable and repeatable.
Not only do we want the mission statement to be clear and concise, but we also want it to be memorable and repeatable. A short, punchy phrase with words that create a picture and evoke emotion help team members embrace and own the mission as well. The sooner team members are repeating the mission statement, the quicker they will internalize and embody it.

It is reinforced by stories.
Great mission statements come to life with stories. Not only do we need to create the mission statement, but team members need to hear the founder's why. If the founder is still a part of your company, he or she needs to be actively sharing

this mission regularly. If your founder is no longer with the company, you want to find a way to capture the founder's story and share it often.

Leaders believe it.

For a mission statement to really take root, every leader at every level needs to believe it. We'll talk more about how to do this in a later chapter. Suffice it to say, if the leaders don't own it, we'll be struggling to get buy-in from others.

HOW CLEAR IS YOUR MISSION?

Odds are you have a mission statement likely written on a wall or buried in the employee handbook. Take it out, dust it off, and confirm your commitment to it. Is it right? Does it reflect the purpose of the organization today? Does the clarity you've created around who you are and how you work together align with the defined mission?

If not, what needs to change? Does your mission need a refresh?

Clarity is the chief indicator of the health of your culture. If the mission feels unclear, your culture will struggle.

Initially Steve's Culture Team didn't think they had a mission statement. As I wrote on the whiteboard, they rattled off a host of statements that they often heard Steve say and they assumed were the mission in different seasons. I happened to glance over at Steve, and I saw a look of confusion. "Steve, what are you thinking right now?" I asked.

"Jenni, I'm honestly so surprised. I thought the mission was clear but I'm realizing that all the different ways that I like to talk about it have created confusion for the team."

At that point, I asked Steve to go to the whiteboard and write out the mission statement. Without a second thought he went to the board and wrote: "To inspire creativity in the heart of every child through exposure to art and beauty."

Immediately the team chimed in:

"Oh yeah, I remember that."

"That's on the wall of our lobby."

"I just wasn't sure if that was still our mission statement."

---

*Clarity is the chief indicator of
the health of your culture.*

What Steve and the team uncovered was that they had a solid mission statement. They had just stopped communicating it effectively and therefore they were lacking alignment around it. This point of clarity got them headed in the right direction.

What I often find as a pleasant by-product of this exploration is that it reconnects you with the heart of your work. So many times, we get busy and distracted by the whirlwind of activity required to keep our organizations moving that we lose sight of why we are here in the first place. Typically, the older your organization is, the more acute this problem will be. The clarity of who you are is critical to a healthy culture. It's all about knowing your *why*.

CULTURE TEAM ACTION PLAN

↳ Review your mission statement together. Is it clear? Is it compelling?

↳ If a mission statement does not exist, you'll want to pause your work to define this. Visit the URL found at the end of the chapter for a mission statement writing exercise.

↳ If your mission exists but needs clarity, invite your senior leader to the conversation to discuss and clarify your mission before you move forward.

WHO YOU ARE

The importance of identity is a popular concept today. Life coaching and life planning are common practice. "Finding yourself" is not an unfamiliar phrase. As a person of faith, I'm a deep believer in the importance of understanding how God has uniquely designed each one of us. One of my favorite scriptures is Galatians 6:4–5: "Make a careful exploration of who you are and the work you have been given, and then sink yourself into that. Don't be impressed with yourself. Don't compare yourself with others. Each of you must take responsibility for doing the creative best you can with your own life." My book *CLOUT: Discover and Unleash Your God-Given Influence*[21] takes a deep dive into this scripture and its application for everyone who wants to be a better steward of their influence. Each one of us has a set of unique gifts, talents, experiences, and opportunities that have shaped our identity. Our job is to uncover and understand them in order to live a life of purpose. That's the power of having clarity around your identity.

This concept also applies to organizations (businesses and nonprofits). Your organization has an identity. There are things that make you unique and distinct. Your corporate identity, so to speak, is a combination of your founder's personality, your history, the experiences that have shaped your organization, and the uniquenesses of the team members assembled to do the work right now.

What is unique or distinct about your organization? Sure, there is another business across town similar to yours, but why do people choose to work with *you*? You might know this instinctively or you might need to spend some time really thinking this through. There are plenty of other organizations that do what you do, but none of them are you. This is the careful exploration that you and the Culture Team need to make. You must move from a vague idea of why you're special to a true understanding of what makes you special. This clarity of who you are is critical for defining your culture.

As Steve's team processed the question "Who are we?" they realized that time and complexity had made this harder to answer. For those who had been there for much of their twenty-five-year history, they could quickly name the distinctives of who they were in the early days. Words like *renegades*, *risk-takers*, *problem-solvers*, and *dreamers* made the top of the list. They admitted they had lost their edge and they set to work to mine for clarity of who they were now.

CULTURE TEAM
ACTION PLAN

Assemble the team to discuss and define who you are:

↳   What do people say about your organization?

- Review your staff survey to look for clues for how the staff talk about the organization. What words or phrases do they use to describe who you are?

- Review customer feedback. What do people note in reviews or customer surveys? If you're a nonprofit or a church, why do your volunteers serve? If you don't have existing mechanisms for this feedback, consider convening a focus group.

- Capture both the positive and negative words or phrases that you see consistently. Use the positive ones to reinforce what's true and what you want to build upon. Use the negative ones to foster conversation about why you're perceived this way and to clarify what you aspire to instead. (The aspiration will become important in Phase 3 of your work).

↳   What does your history say about you?

- What are the stories of your culture? Consider the legends and stories from the early days.

What do those stories tell you about what makes you distinct?

↳ What does your language say about you?

- What is the language of your culture? What are the phrases/axioms you always say?

↳ What has most influenced you?

- What books, leaders, or resources have shaped your thinking as an organization? Most leaders can point to one or two books or authors they most frequently quote. Is there a book that shaped the early culture of your organization? What clues does this give you about your culture?

↳ What is the best of your culture that you want to continue to shape your future?

- Choose three adjectives that describe your culture at its best.
- What stories need to be told to every team member?
- What words or phrases do you need to reinforce in your culture?
- What words or phrases do you need to eliminate from your culture?
- What books or resources does every team member need to read to understand your culture?

CREATE YOUR *WHO WE ARE* STATEMENT

From these discussions and observations from feedback, craft a statement that defines your team at your best.

Who We Are Statement Formula:

We are a [adjective], [adjective], and [adjective] team committed to [insert mission statement].

CLARITY CHECK

	Yes	No
We have a clear, concise, and memorable mission statement.	☐	☐
We can articulate who we are in three words.	☐	☐
We have a strong *Who We Are* statement.	☐	☐

Go to culturemattersbook.com/resources for additional resources from this chapter.

5

Identifying the Gaps in Employee Needs

"There's no magic formula for great company culture. The key is just to treat your staff how you would like to be treated."

—**Richard Branson**[22]

ow do you work together?" When I posed this question to Steve's team I got a deer-in-the-headlights look in response. Admittedly, it's kind of a funny question to answer.

Elizabeth jumped in and started talking about everyone's roles and responsibilities. Tim told me about their meeting structure. But when they recognized that I was looking for more, they were perplexed.

This is when I engaged Sam, the new employee in the room, and asked him about his experience. I asked questions like:

- Based upon what you've experienced working with this team, what would you say is important here?
- What has been surprising or unexpected?
- What gets prioritized?
- Did you do something in your first few days/weeks that you realized is frowned upon in this culture?
- What is different (positive or negative) from your last workplace?

After already having spent most of the day in brave conversations, it seemed Sam felt comfortable enough to be honest and we gleaned some valuable insights. He shared that while leaders say creativity is important, schedules are so full that there is little room for creative discussions to take place. In his opinion they valued efficiency over creativity. He also noted that while there is an org chart that defines roles and responsibilities, not everyone is empowered equally. While one person might be the department leader, there is a legacy employee that everyone goes to for a final decision. He expressed that this was really confusing, especially at first. On the positive side, he shared that team members genuinely care for one another. When they ask how you're doing, they are really interested. This was starkly different, in the best way, from his previous job.

HOW WE WORK TOGETHER

Now that we had surfaced some anecdotal insights about how this team works together, it was time to dive deeper in the Culture Hierarchy of Needs.

The Culture Hierarchy of Needs gives us the roadmap for defining how we work together. The survey in the assessment phase helped us address where gaps may exist in these stages. Now it's time to further understand and define what we need to provide to foster engagement at all levels for all employees.

What is it like to be a part of your team? How do you work together? Asking a new employee about their experience with your organization can be incredibly helpful. If you can get a new employee to be brutally honest about what they experience, you'll glean some very insightful information. The challenge for leaders is that 1) we hold greater responsibility for "how we do things here," so it's harder to admit when it's not great, and 2) this is the culture we know and are comfortable with, so we don't know if there could be something better.

How do we work together? is an incredibly important and powerful question to ask. And answering it is what begins to set the foundation for unlocking your culture.

CULTURE HIERARCHY OF NEEDS

PERSONAL FULFILLMENT

CONNECTION

PSYCHOLOGICAL SAFETY

ORGANIZATIONAL CLARITY

BASIC NEEDS

© Jenni Catron

BASIC NEEDS

Thirty-three percent of employees quit their new job within ninety days, and 32 percent name company culture as the reason for leaving.[23] These disheartening stats only reinforce the fact that equipping new employees for success is extraordinarily critical.

Think about your first day at a new job. No matter how excited you were about the opportunity or how confident you felt in your abilities, the unknowns were overwhelming. Sure, you did your due diligence in interviewing the organization just as they interviewed you, but it's impossible to anticipate every nuance of a new experience.

Every new employee is reduced to baseline needs when they take a new job or even assume a new role within the same organization. This is the basic needs level of the Culture Hierarchy of Needs. This is the foundational level of employee engagement, but oftentimes in our hurriedness we as leaders overlook the importance of it. The longer you've been a part of the organization, the more you take for granted the basics of "how we do things here." When we fail to set new employees up with these basic needs, we create a deficit of knowledge and learning that can be detrimental to their long-term success.

For most employees it takes at least six months to get acclimated to their new role and the culture of the organization, and within that time they are determining whether this is the right place for them. Not only is this level critical for the employee, but it's also enormously critical to the organization. The cost of turnover is tremendous, not only in hard costs associated with interviewing, hiring, training, and onboarding, but also in the less measurable cost of how onboarding a new person affects everyone on the team. Every person connected to the role feels the strain of losing a key team member and their organizational knowledge, as well as the impact from the time it takes to align a new person to your cultural norms.

This level of the hierarchy is about equipping employees with the basic tools they need to know how to effectively contribute to your organization. This includes:

- Clarity of purpose
- Fair compensation
- Onboarding to culture and systems

- Practical tools for their role
- Training and development

Clarity of Purpose

Business and leadership author and speaker Simon Sinek wisely taught us to start with *why*. From an organizational perspective I can't think of much that is more important than making sure every person on your team understands your organization's why. Clarity of purpose means explaining why your organization exists. It's the combination of the mission statement and the "who we are" statements that you defined in the previous chapter. Every team member needs to understand your purpose, which requires you to have a way of communicating it consistently. (In chapter 8 we'll talk about creating a plan for integrating your why into the rhythms of your organization.)

Extensive research repeatedly indicates that having a sense of purpose for their work is the greatest need acknowledged by employees. In O.C. Tanner's "5 Culture Trends for 2023," they cited, "Employees want more from work. More than a high salary or unique perks and benefits, they want the sense of fulfillment that comes from doing work that has a purpose and feeling that they belong to their workplace community."[24]

We set the stage for purpose in this very first level of engagement. Our job at this level is to be extraordinarily clear about the mission of the organization. It's our job to be unapologetic about our why and help the employee see how their role contributes to the big picture.

This clarity of purpose helps employees see their place in the organization and it also helps them verify that the organization's purpose aligns with their own personal mission. If there is misalignment between an employee's passions and the organization's mission, it's better to identify that early. I've seen far too many leaders appeal to an employee's interests in an effort to recruit them, only to create frustration once the organization's mission becomes clear.

Compensation

Money matters. It is a basic need and no matter how amazing your mission is, if your team can't pay their bills, they will be distracted and ultimately resentful. Organizations need great people, and great people need to be honored with fair compensation.

I was recently working with an organization that was reeling from significant staff turnover and an abysmal employee engagement survey. The leaders struggled to understand why the culture was so bad. The camaraderie and connection of the team was great, and as a nonprofit, team members really believed in the purpose of the organization. The senior leaders couldn't understand what was causing the constant turnover and disengagement. As I asked some probing questions and dug deeper into the data, I discovered that this organization had not given any raises for over five years. No cost-of-living adjustments, no merit increases, nothing. A lack of awareness of a very basic need was resulting in far greater cost to the organization.

Payroll is easily the largest operational budget line for most organizations, business or nonprofit. And this is precisely why it is so foundational for organizational culture. While our initial instinct is to keep compensation as low as possible, we must evaluate the broader financial impact of our compensation decisions.

Consider this: The more competitively you pay your employees, the better employees you'll attract and retain. The more employees you retain, the lower your costs of turnover; the lower your turnover costs, the more margin you have to provide raises that enable you to continue to retain those employees. The less turnover you have in your organization, the more institutional knowledge you keep; the more institutional knowledge you keep, the less cost you have in onboarding and training new team members.

Now, let's consider the reverse: The less you pay your employees, the less qualified or talented employees you'll attract. The less qualified your employees are, the more turnover you'll see; the more turnover you have, the greater your costs in hiring. The more costs in hiring, the less resources you have to provide raises; the fewer raises you're giving, the more turnover you'll see with tenured staff. With less tenured staff, you lack institutional knowledge that leads to errors that in turn create additional costs; those additional costs keep you from compensating and training well.

It's a vicious cycle that can be either extraordinarily positive or terribly destructive.

According to the Society for Human Resource Management (SHRM), the cost of losing an employee can be up to double that employee's annual salary, depending on the type of role and their level of experience.

Here's the bottom line: compensation communicates care to your team. A competitive salary with reasonable benefits speaks volumes to your team about how you value them and their families.

As leaders, we can get unnecessarily distracted by the sticker shock of salaries and benefits and miss the forest for the trees. While we of course need to manage the budget wisely and have good benchmarks for how compensation fits in our overall budget strategy, we must guard against having a scarcity mindset when it comes to compensation. Many leaders I know approach hiring or pay increases with an attitude of "How cheap can we get them (or keep them)?" If this is the value by which you're making compensation decisions, your team will feel this. Our values guide us. If your driving value is to get something for nothing, your team will know, and it will impact their level of trust with you.

Here's the bottom line: compensation communicates care to your team.

With all of that said, there will be times when budgets are lean, your organization did not meet projections or funding goals, and you truly can't provide raises, or perhaps you even have to cut jobs. In these situations, you must be honest with your team about the reality.

In 2010, I was working at a nonprofit in Nashville, Tennessee. This was the year of the historic one-thousand-year flood that devastated Middle Tennessee. Thousands of people lost their homes, including three of my staff. As you can imagine, donations were down that year and the budget was tight. We were trying to do as much as we possibly could to help those who lost everything while also trying to keep the lights on and everyone on payroll.

At one point, a team member got frustrated with me because I was saying no to a lot of financial requests. What I thought was an obvious strain on our resources was not obvious to this team member. That was when I realized I needed to be more transparent with the team about our reality. While every person on that team deserved a raise for how hard they worked that year, we were fortunate that we didn't have to cut any jobs due to the circumstances.

What employees really want to know is that the organization has their best interests at heart, that their leaders see the work they're doing and have a desire to compensate them well. These micro moments of clarity are building trust that is essential to the foundation of great teams.

If you're cheap, employees know it and they won't trust you. A culture with a scarcity mindset breeds scarcity. A culture with a generosity mindset breeds generosity.

Onboarding

After about a decade of working for one company, I was making a big leap to a new organization in a completely different industry. I was excited, terrified, and questioning my decision at every turn. Starting a new job is stressful. In conversations before I started, the new organization sent me options for my new laptop. Not only was I getting a brand-new laptop, but they were also giving me a couple of options to choose from. I was overwhelmed by their generosity. My previous company was notorious for recycling and fixing old computers and I was not accustomed to having a new computer that didn't take ten minutes to boot up. Whether they realized it or not, the new company communicated to me that I was important to them. Their generosity communicated respect and value before I was even contributing.

Compare this experience with a story I heard from another new employee at a different company. Ashley arrived at her new organization excited and eager to begin her first day. However, when she arrived, no one was there. After graciously waiting a few minutes and well past the official start of office hours (which were clearly posted on the office door), she called her new boss to see if she had misunderstood her start date or time. When her boss answered the phone, he was distracted and began offering a number of excuses. He thought someone else would be there to meet her; he was on a video call at the moment with the rest of the executive team . . . and today was actually a work-from-home day for all the staff. Instantly, Ashley went from being excited about her new job to feeling like she wasn't important enough for her boss or organization to help her get off to a great start.

A new employee's first experiences with your organization are foundational to their success. They are forming their first impressions of the culture and quickly learning the values, beliefs, and behaviors that are important to you.

In Ashley's case, she likely made the following assumptions from her experience on her first day:

- This team is disorganized.
- They don't communicate well.
- My new boss doesn't value me.
- My role must not be that important.
- You have to fend for yourself here.

Knowing the leaders Ashley works for, I'm confident this is not at all what they wanted her to experience but because they hadn't considered how critical onboarding is to an employee's long-term engagement, they did not realize what they were communicating to her by not being prepared for her first day.

You can make sure that staff members have their basic needs met by ensuring they are adequately equipped and trained when they begin.

Effective onboarding includes:

- Clear communication on their first day
- Having a plan for their first few hours or days
- Introductions to staff
- Extended time with their manager
- A workspace that is prepared and ready for them
- Introduction and training on systems and processes
- Equipped with keys and access codes
- Overview of the employee handbook
- Introduction to your values grid (more on this in chapter 6)

There are many different things you can do to effectively onboard a team member; we'll talk about more specific ideas in chapter 8. The key to onboarding a team member well is in demonstrating to them that they are a priority by having a clear plan and giving them the appropriate time and information that sets them up well.

A new employee's first days should be an immersion in who you are and how you work together. They should see your values in action and be reassured they made a great decision in coming to work here.

Practical Tools for Their Role

In the popular Apple TV sitcom *Ted Lasso*, an American football coach is recruited to coach an English football (soccer) club. As an outsider, Ted has a lot of work ahead of him to build trust with the team. To get early input from the team, Ted creates a suggestion box. One of the comments in the suggestion box is about the poor water pressure in the showers. A few days later the somewhat ornery captain of the team is taking a shower and discovers vastly improved water pressure. Simple attention to a practical need earns Ted some much-needed trust with the team. He eliminates a distraction so they could focus on the more critical issues in front of them.

Equipping your team with practical tools is about making sure team members have the basic tools to do their job. Are you equipping your team with what they need to do their job in today's environment?

Historically this would have meant equipping them with computers that work, adequate space and time to do their work, and appropriate compensation. Today, this may also mean accommodations for flexible work schedules.

Employees need to be equipped with the practical tools to do their job. This includes:

- Computer or laptop and appropriate software
- Keys and access codes
- Office space (if applicable) that is commensurate with the type of work they do and the amount of time they are expected to be in the office
- Clarity on work-from-home policies
- Training on organizational systems and processes

In addition to setting new employees up for success, you set and maintain a good foundation for team members when they aren't inhibited by ineffective equipment. When team members have to beg for a new computer or software to do their work, they feel devalued. This becomes especially critical if new employees get all the new equipment, but long-tenured staff get hand-me-downs.

The frustration of not having good working equipment bogs team members down both mentally and physically. The frustration they carry impedes their work, and the additional time it takes to work with poor equipment costs both time and mental energy.

I also want to acknowledge that you will have team members who always want the newest gadget or most recent technology; this is especially common for team members in production, IT, or creative roles. These are the innovators in your organization, and they are enamored by the newest and brightest options on the market. In this case, it's a tension to manage and requires listening for and understanding their true needs versus wants. Don't quickly dismiss their latest request but also don't blindly approve everything they lobby for.

The best solution for finding a healthy balance for providing the practical tools that employees need is to set parameters for what you provide and how frequently you replace it. These standards clarify expectations and create consistency, both of which foster trust. Here again, err on the side of generosity. It will serve you well and it will pay off. When team members lack the tools they need, they can be easily frustrated and become disengaged. The cost of retaining a great staff member far outweighs the few dollars you saved by keeping that computer an extra year or not replacing that broken office chair.

Training & Development

My first real job post-college was my dream job. Ever since I was thirteen years old, I had wanted to work for ForeFront Records, and when I was twenty, I landed an internship with the company. I was quickly hired and promoted but was incredibly inexperienced. ForeFront was a division of EMI Music, which at the time was the leading record company in the world and had a robust corporate infrastructure including a stellar HR team and a rigorous training and development program. A few years ago, I stumbled upon my certificate of completion for EMI University, which was an extended training program for new managers in the company. Little did I know at the time how valuable this investment would be and how much it would shape my future. Their investment in me created a lifetime commitment to growth and the importance of developing talent.

The cornerstone of this first level of the culture hierarchy is your commitment to the continued training and development of your team. Being intentional to develop your team communicates enormous value. And while I believe every person must ultimately own their growth and development, organizations that create opportunities for development have greater engagement and retention. According to research from Gallup, "Organizations that have made a strategic investment in employee development report 11% greater profitability and are twice as likely to retain their employees."[25]

To grow with your organization, your team needs to be constantly learning. Your investment in them is also an investment in the future of your organization.

Training for your team may include:

- Specific skills training and/or professional development related to their role
- Training on your organizational values and what they look like in action
- Ongoing leadership skills training
- Cross-departmental mentoring
- Professional leadership coaching

Commitment to personal and professional growth communicates that you value the bettering of each team member. Your investment in their development indicates your commitment to them personally. When employees are a part of an organization that values investing in them, their commitment level and loyalty go up.

SET THE FOUNDATION

Since Sam had shared such helpful insights about his experience as the newest employee, the Culture Team was eager to hear his observations on the Basic Needs level of the hierarchy. They all had a sinking suspicion that there were some gaps in the onboarding experience. As Sam shared, they took notes and captured ideas for what they could improve upon.

In a lull in the conversation, Tim, the operations director, opened the discussion about compensation. He was already feeling a little anxious about the topic and figured it would be better to just dive in. "Okay, team . . . I'll admit as the one responsible for overseeing the budget, I know that I have had a tendency to be frugal with payroll and have probably made some of you nervous to bring up this part of the discussion. First, I want to say that I'm sorry for creating that atmosphere and second, I sincerely want to hear your observations and recommendations for how we can fairly compensate our team."

As they continued their discussion, I couldn't help but smile. This team was having the right and honest conversations about their culture, and I knew their work was going to pay off.

These foundational elements of the hierarchy, while seemingly simple, are extraordinarily critical in building a foundation of trust. Purpose, compensation, basic tools, onboarding, and training seem obvious at first glance, but perhaps because they seem obvious many leaders are tempted to overlook the importance of them.

When team members are distracted because they don't have appropriate tools to do their work, it becomes difficult for them to contribute at a higher level. When our basic needs aren't met, we're fighting for survival rather than focusing on achieving the mission.

Now, I know what you may be thinking: *We don't have the budget for all the latest gadgets that my team members want.* I get that, but I'm not talking about extravagance. What is important is that we truly understand what our team members need and are consciously ensuring that we're not unintentionally frustrating and inhibiting them from doing their best work.

When our basic needs aren't met, we're fighting for survival rather than focusing on achieving the mission.

CULTURE TEAM
ACTION PLAN

↳ Review these key components of the Basic Needs level of the hierarchy.

↳ Discuss areas of weakness and strength.

↳ Brainstorm ways that you could immediately improve upon the early experience for new employees.

In chapter 8, you'll revisit these ideas and build your plan to address them.

CLARITY CHECK

	Yes	No
Our employees understand our purpose.	☐	☐
We compensate our team appropriately.	☐	☐
We have a consistent onboarding plan.	☐	☐
We adequately equip our team with the tools for their role.	☐	☐
We have a plan for training and development.	☐	☐

6

Clarifying How You Work Together

"The most important thing to understand about transforming a culture, whether that of a team or a whole company, is that it isn't a matter of simply professing a set of values and operating principles. It's a matter of identifying the behaviors that you would like to see become consistent practices and then instilling the discipline of actually doing them."

—Patty McCord[26]

What would Steve want?"

As I worked with Steve's team, I heard this question frequently. They didn't feel confident in a direction unless Steve had spoken into it. This is not uncommon, especially for founder-led organizations. In young, growing organizations, the leader's instincts are essential for direction and often survival, but as the organization grows, it's impossible (and unhealthy) to sustain. While there may be a number of reasons for a culture where the senior leader feels the need to speak into every decision (anxiety, control, mistrust), the issue at the heart in this case was values. Steve operated from a set of strongly held values and convictions that guided his decision-making. The problem was that he had not articulated them—to himself or to the team. It didn't matter if they were making a decision about a major strategic initiative or the color of the baseboards in the new building; Steve had a strong "gut" reaction and if the team didn't guess correctly what Steve's "gut" would be, they often had to redirect or redo the work, causing significant frustration. Even the most tenured team members had trouble predicting what he wanted, and it stemmed from a lack of clarity around values. They didn't have an understanding of the guiding principles that informed his decision-making and as a result all decisions had to be directed to Steve. With over one hundred employees, this was not realistic or sustainable.

DEFINING ORGANIZATIONAL CLARITY

As you seek to define your culture, the organizational clarity level of the hierarchy becomes an important guide for what needs to be defined.

© Jenni Catron

Now that we've acknowledged the basic needs employees have, we move to what I believe is the most critical level of the culture hierarchy: organizational clarity. This second level of the hierarchy is the single greatest differentiator between extraordinary teams and mediocre teams. I cannot overemphasize the power of this need. It's essentially the crux of culture. In fact, in an assessment that thousands of leaders have taken on the 4Sight website,[27] over 66 percent identified this level of the hierarchy as the hindrance in their culture.

Because this is such an important part of establishing a healthy culture, I've devoted two chapters to organizational clarity. In this chapter we're going to look at values. In the next chapter we'll discuss vision, strategy, structure, roles, and responsibilities.

What I most want you to take away from these chapters is less about the specific process I share for each of these things (in fact, I do my best to not get terribly in the weeds on how), but more so, I want you to understand exactly why these elements of organizational clarity are so essential to building an extraordinary team.

Clarity is a chief indicator of the health of a culture. Show me a team that . . .

- understands the vision,
- has a strategy for achieving it,
- can articulate the values that guide how they work together,
- has a structure for how they work together,
- understands their specific roles and responsibilities for executing toward the mission,

. . . and I'm confident you'll see a team where every member is thriving and engaged.

Here is the challenge: If you're the leader, these elements of organizational clarity likely feel clear to you. We undervalue and underestimate their impact because they are not a perceived need of ours. We often don't understand the confusion that a lack of clarity creates throughout the organization.

Clarity at this stage will be the game changer in building a culture that is aligned and working effectively to achieve mission.

BUILDING YOUR VALUES GRID

What lives underneath all the activity your team does day to day is a value structure that has been instilled in the system, typically without conscious acknowledgment. Your team has a value structure even if you have never done the work of writing a set of values. In fact, even if you have done the work of crafting values, it was likely a very episodic event influenced by values you perceived as the right ones to have. As a result, it became a corporate exercise that was disconnected from who you are.

Crafting your team's values is the single greatest thing you can do to define how your team works together.

If I asked you the question, "What does your team look like at its best?" you would quickly rattle off a string of adjectives and be beaming with pride as you share them. However, if I asked you what your team values, you'll probably stall for a minute trying to recall that document that you created from a workshop several years ago. At best, you'll reference a list of corporate-sounding buzzwords that hang on the wall in your lobby.

Crafting your team's values is the single greatest thing you can do to define how your team works together.

Strong, clearly defined values:

- Provide a filter for decision-making
- Clarify expectations
- Give team members confidence in what is expected from them
- Simplify the need for bureaucracy

Values are a set of guiding principles that clarify the habits and behaviors that are essential to accomplishing your mission.

Values are the anchor that holds your team together when everything else feels uncertain. During the global pandemic of 2020 when every organization was adrift trying to figure out how to survive in a volatile and unpredictable market, values were what held together the best teams. The pressure of the pandemic obliterated our strategies, quickly eroded our team culture with the demands of remote work, and forced us to revisit the question of purpose: Why do we do what we do? What held the best teams together despite these uncertainties were the values that guided them.

Values answer the question of "how?" How will we work together, lead together, accomplish mission together in both the familiar and unexpected? How will we make decisions? How will we behave in a way that is congruent with our purpose and accomplishes our strategy?

Values are the linchpin to organizational life but are often quite difficult for us to define in a way that is memorable and, more importantly, impactful. Whether stated or not, you have values. There are guiding principles that are driving how your team works together. The bigger question is, are your values producing the results you want?

Defining your values is the next and arguably most important part of the LeadCulture Framework.

VALUES ALONE ARE NOT ENOUGH

"Can I be honest?" Greg spoke up. The team nodded enthusiastically. Greg had been one of the quieter team members so far in the process and the others were eager to hear his thoughts. Although he was trying to temper his emotion, you couldn't deny the exasperation in his next question: "Haven't we done numerous rounds of staff values through the years? I don't really see the point. They haven't worked for us in the past. Why will they work now?"

"That's not entirely true," Elizabeth responded a bit defensively. "We put a lot of time into that last version of staff values, and I think we did really good work."

"Well, honestly, Elizabeth, I know you personally put a lot of effort into those values, but I bet not a single person in this room could tell you what they are. I don't mean to frustrate you and I mean no disrespect to Jenni, but this feels like a waste of our time." And with that, Greg slumped back in his chair.

It was clear the room was a little uncomfortable. Quickly Alli chimed in, perhaps concerned for mine and Elizabeth's feelings. "Maybe we just didn't have the right values in the past. I'm sure this time will be better."

Before other team members had a chance to try to diffuse the tension, I spoke up. "Actually, Greg, you raise a really important point. Thank you for being willing to ask the difficult question. Our culture gets better when we are willing to be honest about what's not working and take action to more deliberately fix it. The wrestling and the respectful debate are really important. Whether you know it or not, you all just took a major step forward in creating a healthy culture . . . but more about that later. Right now, we need to wrestle down this disagreement over the importance of values."

Writing values has been so overemphasized in organizational best practices that the novelty has worn off. We've dismissed their effectiveness because it seems they have had little effect on the actual performance of some of the companies that proudly displayed them. Perhaps the most obvious and cringeworthy example is the infamous Enron scandal with their values of Integrity, Communication, Respect, and Excellence proudly displayed in the corporate office lobby. ("The company hid massive trading losses, ultimately leading to one of the largest accounting scandals and bankruptcy in recent history."[28]) Sadly, many more examples like this exist, just on a much smaller scale.

It's not enough to simply define values. There is a deeper level of clarity required to anchor your values in your culture in such a way that they truly inform how you work together.

For the remainder of this chapter, I'm going to teach you how to develop your values grid. Your values grid is a tool to equip your team to truly understand your values and how to live into them.

The values grid is comprised of four elements:

1. The value itself
2. The belief behind that value
3. The behaviors that reflect that value
4. The "sticky statement" or the internal language and/or stories that make that value unique to your team

PROBLEMS WITH YOUR VALUES

The problem for Steve and his team was that they actually had two sets of values. They had the values that were on the wall, and they had the way things really got done within the organization. Oftentimes these values felt at odds. What often won out in their culture were the unwritten values, which were arbitrary and unclear.

Let's talk about the typical problems with values:

No one pays attention to them.
You may have stated values that are beautifully written and hang on the wall of your organization, but no one actually knows or pays attention to them. And more critically, your habits and behaviors don't reflect them. These values have had little to no effect on your day-to-day interactions as a team. They were an exercise you checked off on "the things that good organizations do" list, but you never really made them a part of your operations, so they don't influence your culture—or at least they don't influence your culture in a

good way. They may actually be a negative in your culture because your team walks by them every day and becomes increasingly cynical of your lack of organizational awareness. You're probably declaring values that most team members don't believe are true of who you are and how you work together to achieve your mission.

Your values are working against you.
Perhaps you don't have stated values, but there are definitely habits and behaviors that influence how your team works together. These are the things that new employees notice. They are either unstated values or accidental values and, if you're honest, they are working against you more than they are working for you. Unstated or accidental values can be both good and bad in nature, but the lack of intentionality in recognizing what you value starts to erode morale.

Unstated values could be:

- Quality—You hold a high standard for quality that is often misunderstood as perfectionism or micromanagement.
- Responsiveness—You expect everyone to respond promptly, and you perceive others as lazy who don't respond as quickly as you think they should.
- Tidiness—Clutter makes you crazy so you are constantly cleaning up after others and getting frustrated at how sloppy they are.

Accidental values could be:

- Lack of accountability—In an effort to be understanding or agreeable, you don't hold team members accountable for what they said they would do.
- Tardiness—Meetings constantly start late so everyone arrives late.
- Perfectionism—Fear of failure creates a culture where anything less than perfect is frowned upon or micromanaged.

The greatest problem with unstated and accidental values is that because they are not identified, they are like land mines. You don't know you've violated a value until you've accidentally stepped on it. The lack of clarity around what's most important in your culture instills fear in team members. They are never quite certain when they are going to misstep.

Creating a shared set of values that align your team is some of the most important work you can do as a leader. One of my favorite parts of the LeadCulture Framework is that of crafting values that provide your team with "rules of engagement" for how you accomplish your vision and goals together.

Values are the guiding principles that tether your team together and will equip your team to become stronger and more unified.

VALUES GRID

The key to writing values that are effective at shaping your culture is to build a framework that provides meaning and depth to the values you've defined. One of key tools of the LeadCulture Framework is the values grid. The values grid provides a framework for your values to live in and creates a level of clarity that makes your values distinct to your team.

A good values grid should be unique to your team. It should have meaning, stories, and language that only insiders know. A strong values grid provides a sense of camaraderie and unity for your team.

When I was first developing the values grid, I was the executive director of a large, multi-site church. We were one of the fastest-growing churches in the country at the time and our team was expanding rapidly. If you had asked me what we valued, I would have shared characteristics that were instinctual to those of us who had been there since the very early days. That's the nature of values that shape culture—as mentioned earlier, in young organizations the values are typically caught, and they usually reflect the values of the founding leader. As long as you have close proximity to the founding or senior leader, savvy team members pick up on the values that guide decision-making and they quickly discern "what's important here."

The problem that I began to notice, and that plagues many teams that have never done the work of defining a values grid, is that it was simply impossible for everyone on the team to "catch" the values. As we grew to twenty, thirty, fifty team members, I couldn't expect everyone to catch what was most important to how we worked together to achieve our mission. This was when it became clear to me that I needed to define a set of values and teach those values to every existing team member and to every new person who would come on board.

Our values grid provided clarity in language, understanding, and behaviors that resulted in greater alignment throughout the organization.

VALUES GRID

VALUE	BELIEF	BEHAVIORS	STICKY STATEMENT /STORIES

© Jenni Catron

WRITING VALUES THAT ARE MORE THAN STATEMENTS ON A WALL

Once we acknowledged the tension around values, I took a few minutes to explain the power of the values grid and shared examples from other teams I had led through the process. I quickly saw Steve's team's interest grow. Even Greg perked up when I said, "Values alone are not enough."

Now the team got to work. Over the next several hours they brainstormed an exhaustive list of possible values and then narrowed it down to five that they agreed were most critical for how their team works together to achieve their mission. Then things started to get fun. We broke up into smaller groups to define beliefs and behaviors to support those values. Finally, they recalled stories and examples that had us laughing hysterically one minute and moved to tears the next. It was clear that we had drafted a set of values that were truly more than statements on a wall.

Here are the four steps of the values grid process:

1. Start simple.

Oftentimes when I'm working with a team on creating their values, they get hung up on getting it perfect right from the start. They've felt the pain of a ho-hum list of values that feel corporate and stuffy, and they desperately want to create something exciting and motivating. I completely understand this pain point and I want to assure you that we'll get to the fun and creative part of the values grid that will make your values come to life for your team. But initially, I want you to start simple.

You don't need to be clever. You don't need to narrow them down. You just need to start brainstorming. Gather your team together and collectively brainstorm the values that you want to be true of how you work together.

Discuss questions like:

- What is important to us?
- What do we want to be true of how we work together?
- What makes our team distinct from another team?
- What phrases do we frequently use to encourage and motivate our team?
- Are there any axioms that have become common language?
- What values did the founder of our organization hold? What was most important to him/her?

If your founder is still your senior leader or an active part of the team, as was the case for Steve's organization, take extra time to capture the values most important to him or her. Oftentimes it will be difficult for leaders to give language to their values because they are so instinctual. Prompt him/her with questions based upon observations you have. For example, in working with Steve I learned through conversations with team members that he would get deep into the details of new building construction. This inevitably caused frustration for his team when he walked into a building and wanted to change the color of the walls. When I probed a bit, I discovered that he held a high value of beauty. He wanted the spaces for their organization to be beautifully designed, and if the color scheme was off, he felt that it impacted the experience for their customers. What was perceived as micromanagement was actually rooted in a really deep value that the team had not fully grasped. With an understanding of his passion for aesthetics, the team gave more priority to this value in their decision-making.

You're hunting for the things that are truly important to you as a team. What makes you different from another similar organization across town? Fill a whiteboard with ideas and then spend some time refining this list. I recommend narrowing it down to three to five values that are most critical for your team to accomplish the mission.

You're probably going to argue that there is no way that you can narrow it down to three to five values but I'm going to challenge you to try. Your goal isn't to capture everything that's important. Your goal is to capture the three to five values that are disproportionately important to who you are as an organization and how your team works together to achieve the mission. (Are you getting tired of me repeating the definition of culture yet?)

It doesn't mean there won't be other things that are important, but you're looking to narrow it down to the three to five that are most distinct to your culture.

For example, character is a value that is important (I hope) to all leaders. I believe that's a "permission to play" value. If you're not already aspiring to lead with great character, you shouldn't have made the team. There will be a number of such values that fall into this category: integrity, honesty, etc. From your brainstorming list, move the expected values to a separate column and then ensure you have a plan in your hiring process to confirm alignment with these values before someone even joins the team.

Now, what you want to look for in the remaining list are the values that are distinct and help clarify why this team culture is different from others. (The work you did in chapter 4 in defining who you are will be valuable to this discussion.)

With your list of three to five values in hand you'll move to the second step in the values grid.

2. Define the belief.

Do you really believe these values matter? The first step was an exercise is capturing your instincts and observations. Now it's time to test the strength of these values by clarifying the belief that supports each one.

Push yourself to consider why these values really matter. Ask questions like:

- Why is each value important?
- Why did that value make it to the final list?
- What's the belief or the core conviction that will cause this value to hold up under pressure?

For example, one of the 4Sight team values is self-leadership. This is based on the belief that we must lead ourselves well in order to lead others better. How can my team and I expect to equip other leaders effectively if we aren't first prioritizing the value of leading ourselves well?

Spend some time talking through each value and why it is significant to your organization in this season, and then craft a belief statement for each value. Capture a one- or two-sentence belief statement that quickly explains why this value matters.

Here's another example.

> *Value*: Collaborative Communication
> *Belief*: Good communication is an act of respect for my coworkers.

That one simple statement provides a very clarifying and compelling why. Everyone wants to be respected, so if you want respect, you must give respect. When we're communicating well, we're respecting others.

3. Clarify the behaviors.

What you value is more about what you do than what you say. It's not enough to come up with team values. You must also define the behaviors that reflect each value. This part of the process begins to unlock your values in a way that brings them to life for your team. Up until now, they are concepts. As you define the behaviors or actions that reflect them, you show your team members how to live into them.

For each value you need to answer the question: What does it look like when our team is working from this value?

This step is super important. Let's say you define a value of responsiveness. Without describing your expectations for what responsiveness looks like, every person on your team will bring their own interpretation to that value. One person might think being responsive means replying to an email whenever they can get to it, while your expectation may be that every team member should respond within an hour.

While it will be impossible to define every behavior that would reflect that value, you want to identify three to five behaviors that represent what that value looks like in action.

For the 4Sight value of self-leadership, a few key behaviors that reflect this value are:

- We establish and maintain healthy rhythms personally and professionally.
- We are committed to consistent growth and learning by pursuing continued education and certifications that help us serve our clients better.
- We pursue relationships with leaders a few steps ahead of us.

Values must be reinforced with behaviors that are consistent and congruent with those values in order to truly be effective.

4. Make your values memorable.

Let's be honest. Your values are probably not going to be so revolutionary that no other team has ever chosen the same ones before, and yet you want to ensure these values are unique to you. This final step in the values grid is where your values get distinct. Along the way you've likely surfaced stories and anecdotes that express the uniqueness of this value for your team.

Now you want to create a "sticky statement" that makes the value memorable. It might be a fun phrase that has become insider language for your team, or it may be based upon a story within your culture.

For example, one of the organizations where I served as executive director had a value of "collaborative communication." Frankly, the value itself is a snoozer. That value could be hanging on every corporate conference room wall. We all want our teams to communicate well, but this value was important to us because communication was getting more and more complex as we added and expanded our locations and staff. The value was highly important. We just needed a clever way to say it.

Ultimately, we landed on the phrase "Use your blinker," based upon a legend in our team culture of my . . . shall we say . . . *efficient* driving style. While you might be holding on for dear life as my passenger, one thing you will notice is that I religiously use my turn signal when I'm driving. If you're going to move fast, you need to communicate well to avoid a crash.

The same intentionality was needed from our team. If we were going to continue to move fast and respond to growth, we needed to be even more deliberate to "use our blinker" and communicate well to one another.

That fun story and powerful visual brought distinctiveness to this value for us. Immediately we all had greater respect for the power of collaborative communication. To this day I still get texts or emails from coworkers from that era that say "using my blinker," indicating that they are sharing information they feel is important for me to know.

The strength of the values grid brought a boring value to life in our organization, and it can do the same for you.

A WORD OF CAUTION

Some of you are going to be tempted to take one of the values grid examples we've provided or values you've seen from another organization you admire and adopt them as your own. I've seen this done time and time again and it's always a colossal failure. The process I've defined above is not just about producing the result. The process itself is refining and clarifying for the entire team and perhaps more importantly for the leader. Every leader has unwritten values that guide their decision-making and leadership style. They make hundreds of decisions every day filtered through those values but often they can't articulate why they liked one choice better than another or why they were so adamant about signing off on the design of a new project.

Many times, when it seems a leader is being hypercontrolling it's because there is an intuitive reaction they are having to decisions they fear others will not catch. Doing the work of extracting your values and then building your belief statements, behaviors, language, and stories helps a leader translate their instinctual responses into a tangible framework that enables the rest of the team to operate in alignment with that leader's instincts. There is no way to fast-track this process. You just need to take the time and commit to the work of defining your values grid.

HOW LONG DO VALUES LAST?

I often get asked how often you should rewrite your values. The answer to this is somewhat subjective, but I do have a few rules of thumb for you to consider. Values will have a shelf life. Your mission is usually timeless, your vision should have a fixed timeline (for example, ten locations in ten years), and your values typically serve you well for a season. This season will often correspond with your vision because they will be the values that are important to help you live out this era of your mission and vision. If I had to put a time frame on it, I would say that values usually serve a team well for seven to ten years.

The key times I recommend an organization revisit their values grid are:

Transition of the most senior leader

When an organization goes through a change in senior leadership, especially the most senior leader, it is appropriate and typically necessary to do a review of the values. While the values reflect the culture of the entire team, key leaders have disproportionate influence on the values that will guide how you work together. Therefore, the senior leader needs to believe in them and embody them.

In most cases, alignment with the values will be a part of the recruiting process; however, it's not uncommon for a new leader to make some adjustments to the values. It's likely that they are casting new vision for the future, and values alignment is critical to their success in leading toward that vision.

If an organization already has a set of values that they have actively engaged, the new senior leader typically just needs to do some refinement or updates. What I often see is a blending of the old values with a few new ones that are important for the season ahead under new leadership.

One organization that I worked with went through a leadership transition about ten years after the initial creation of their staff values. Once the new leader arrived, the team spent a day revisiting their values. They gave the new leader the history of the existing set of values and then as a team they discussed which ones felt most critical for the future. Additionally, they discussed other values that might need to be added. After some healthy debate and discussion, they ended up removing one value and adding a new one. The resulting set of values was a beautiful blend of their history coupled with a new value that was critical to carrying out their new vision.

Major shift in mission, vision, or strategy
Much like the above, a major change in mission, vision, or strategy creates an important inflection point for revisiting your values. Values are a set of guiding principles that clarify the habits and behaviors that are essential to accomplishing your mission and vision. When the mission or vision changes, it stands to reason that your values should be revisited.

A small business that I consulted with recently made some significant changes in their office rhythms. Where they used to require employees to be full-time in the office, they made adjustments to allow for remote and hybrid work. This was a key strategy for employee recruitment and retention. After a few months of adjusting to their new work rhythms, they realized they needed to revisit their values. Many of their values assumed in-person interaction and they needed to elevate values that fostered communication and collaboration in a virtual context. While the values themselves didn't change, they refined their behaviors to better reflect their new strategy.

It's not enough to define some values and throw them on the wall. What gives your values meaning and distinctiveness is the significance of the values to your culture. What you value is important. Defining the values that drive behavior, influence your decisions, and equip your team to move forward is a critical part of leading with clarity.

CULTURE TEAM
ACTION PLAN

↳   Follow the four steps for writing values and create your values grid.

↳   This will likely take several sessions so be patient with the process and keep refining until it provides the clarity your team needs to better understand how you work together.

CLARITY CHECK

	Yes	No
We have a set of organizational values.	☐	☐
We have written belief statements for our values.	☐	☐
We have defined behaviors for our values.	☐	☐
We have memorable language and/or stories for our values.	☐	☐
Our team know our values.	☐	☐
Our values guide our decision-making.	☐	☐

Go to culturemattersbook.com/resources for additional resources from this chapter.

7

Creating Clarity
That Builds Trust

"Clarity creates an organizational road
map to success. It drives faster and better
decision-making while increasing trust."
—Tim Leman[29]

The values work was a game changer for Steve and his
team. So many things that felt confusing and incon-
sistent began to make sense as they extracted the values
that were informing decision-making, especially around
Steve's instincts. As we were evaluating our work and discussing the impact on the organization, Lucy, one of the
long-tenured team members, spoke up: "This is so valuable
in helping us know how to make decisions as a team, but I

still don't know *who* makes decisions." Immediately the rest of the team exhaled an exasperated "Yeessssss!" in unison. They had identified the next big piece of the organizational clarity part of the hierarchy.

They were unearthing a truth that many leaders overlook: we are never as clear as we think we are.

When you hear the word *clarity*, what do you think of? For most people we typically assume communication, but organizational clarity is far more than just communication (we'll get to that later). Organizational clarity requires a fierce commitment to making sure our systems and processes provide the clarity and alignment that removes roadblocks and helps our team do their work with minimal avoidable frustration.

When people are unsure about how their role supports the vision, when they feel their time is being wasted in ineffective meetings, and when they feel confusion about priorities, they will quickly become disengaged. You have the opportunity to address the systems and processes that can make your organization effective and purposeful.

THE FIGHT FOR CLARITY

The year 2019 was an amazing year for strategic planning. Every organization I worked with was nearly salivating at the opportunity to create their 2020 Vision for the upcoming year—the play on words (or numbers if you will) was too good to pass up. As 2020 started, leaders shared these visions with great enthusiasm and confidence—and then on the fateful day of March 14, every grand vision was abandoned as we dealt with extraordinary upheaval brought on by the global COVID-19 pandemic. Those grand visions and strategies quickly became a thing of the past as we wrestled with questions of survival. How do we continue to do business? How do we serve our customers while maintaining a safe distance? How do we successfully work from home?

For many months, we focused on what was immediately in front of us, reacting to our circumstances the best we could. Over the next couple of years, we continued to get back to a sense of normalcy, but I noticed one thing that was particularly lagging: our desire to cast a vision for the future.

I'm not a psychologist but if I had to guess, I would say that most leaders were either nervous to attempt to define a vision for the future since their grand 2020 visions were such a flop and/or they were struggling to see a future state. Employers and employees spent so much time reacting to their circumstances that getting back to proactive posture was quite challenging.

What I began to notice in my work with organizations was that leaders were stuck, and team members were frustrated because they lacked a vision for the future.

VISION IS YOUR WHAT

Vision inspires hope. If your mission is your why, the vision is your what—a more specific target defining what it will take to bring that mission to life. A vision is essentially a large, audacious goal in the future that helps us measure how we're going to live out the mission.

For example:

4Sight Mission: to cultivate healthy leaders to leading thriving teams

4Sight Vision: to coach and equip 100,000 leaders in 3 years

The vision gives my team a specific and measurable target to shoot for that is in support of our mission.

Missions are lofty, idealistic statements of purpose that are inspiring but often difficult to know how to act upon. Visions begin to provide a picture of what that mission looks like within a more specific time frame. The reason this is so critical for team members is that they can't hit a target that hasn't been defined. They need a big goal to both excite and motivate them.

Team members join for our why—our mission—but they engage because of our what—our vision.

STRATEGY IS YOUR HOW

With a vision defined, it's time to get more specific about how you'll achieve that vision. While a vision is exciting and motivating, it can also quickly be overwhelming if team members can't tie their daily actions to the vision.

This is the power of a strategic plan. A strategic plan starts with the mission and vision and then defines strategies, tactics, and actions required to put feet to this vision. It's essentially a tool to help every person on the team know specifically what to do today to help them achieve the vision tomorrow.

While Steve's Culture Team was chomping at the bit to talk about roles, I slowed us down a minute to do a clarity check on vision and strategy.

"This makes so much sense," Tim piped up. "We had to radically change our strategy, merge some locations, and approach our work completely differently in order to survive. We all understood that and made the necessary changes, but we didn't really recast the vision around it. I think we kind of intuitively have an understanding, but I think we need to talk more openly about our vision now."

Everyone in the room nodded enthusiastically. They recognized that they needed to state the vision more clearly and confirm the strategy to support it to bring clarity to everyone's roles and responsibilities now. I could see it was making sense. They were connecting the dots and now we were ready to talk about my favorite thing—org charts!

CLARITY. CLARITY. CLARITY.

I'm a Wisconsin girl and by default, a Green Bay Packers fan. The Packers' history is an ongoing story of the power of a great team. The Packers franchise is an underdog in every sense of the term. Green Bay is the smallest city to ever have an NFL team. Founded in a community that is not large enough to have the necessary infrastructure to host major sporting events, Lambeau Field is one of the most iconic stadiums in the sport.

The 2023–24 season for Green Bay was a year of rebuilding. After eighteen seasons, longtime quarterback Aaron Rogers left the team, and loyal Packers fans watched, sometimes in agony, as a new team had to figure out their roles and responsibilities. The first half of the regular season they had three wins and six losses; the second half of the season they had six wins and three losses. What we witnessed every week was a team that was fighting for clarity for who was doing what now and how they work together in the new structure. Essentially, they were rebuilding their culture, bringing clarity to who they are and how they work together to achieve their mission.

Throughout the season, I found myself more and more invested in their success because I saw them fighting for the clarity that leads to success. That's what this stage of the hierarchy is all about.

Clarity. Clarity. Clarity.

With significant shifts in staffing, the Packers had to reorganize. It was essential that they bring clarity to their roles and responsibilities to reflect who is doing what now. Without this level of clarity, the team would be a chaotic mess on the field.

The same is true for your team.

ORGANIZATIONAL STRUCTURE

I love a good org chart. Give me your org chart and I'll tell you within two minutes how effective your team is. Growth consultant Les McKeown says that your organizational chart is your team's "decision-making tool." A good org chart helps everyone understand their place on the team. Essentially it clarifies *their* purpose in helping the organization accomplish *its* purpose.

Chief among the issues that create a lack of organizational clarity is a nonexistent or confusing organizational chart. Many senior leaders I talk to get annoyed by the desire for an org chart. They often don't feel the need for an org chart because they likely sit somewhere near the top of it. It's clear to them and therefore they assume it's clear for everyone.

But for as powerful as organizational structures can be, I often hear, "We don't really have one," "We have one but it's not really how we work," "It's out of date," or "Nobody ever uses it."

Do those excuses sound familiar?

A well-designed organizational structure serves two important purposes:

1. It equips you to execute your mission, vision, and strategy.

   This first part is critical. Your organizational structure should be designed to support your strategy. They are completely interconnected. In fact, whenever your mission, vision, and strategy change, you should be revisiting your org chart. Misaligned org charts are where I see the most ineffective use of employee time and organizational resources.

2. It helps everyone understand their place.

   This second point is really meaningful. If you've designed an org chart that supports your strategy to accomplish your vision and mission, every role becomes essential. When you've connected the dots from my role on the team to how it helps us achieve the mission of the organization, immediately I see purpose and value in my contribution. I know that my role and responsibilities matter. This understanding and awareness is a powerful part of setting the foundation for team members to find fulfillment in their work. They are gaining confidence and trust in the value of their contribution.

Key characteristics of a good org chart:

- It exists, not just in a leader's mind but in an actual document that all staff are familiar with.
- It can be quickly understood without explanation.

Most leaders and organizations adopt whatever has existed in their history and continue to make slight modifications based upon who is on the team. Essentially what ends up happening is you have a convoluted mess of lines and boxes reflecting who is on the team and who they report to but with no real connection to your strategy or your mission.

If you don't understand your org chart, I guarantee your team doesn't understand it either.

THE STARTING POINT OF BUILDING A GOOD ORG CHART

Many leaders approach their org chart by first looking at who is on the team and considering how best to organize them according to their talents or interests and/or who they get along with.

This approach prioritizes the people over the mission and while that sounds like a great philosophy, especially in a book about the importance of team culture, this is actually the exact opposite of how you should approach structuring your team.

As a leader, you hold two responsibilities, in this order:

1. To fulfill the mission and vision of your organization
2. To align a team of talented staff to achieve that mission and vision

The second is subservient to the first because without a mission, there isn't work for a team to accomplish. The great challenge for most leaders is to hold these two priorities in appropriate balance.

The better way to design your organizational chart is to think first what, then who.

WHAT, THEN WHO STRUCTURE

The primary purpose of your organizational chart is to organize your team to achieve your mission. Your mission is the anchor that you come back to time and time again. As previously mentioned, your mission also needs a strategy to help you achieve it. That strategy is your guide to designing your organizational structure.

Allow me to pause here to note why organizational structures can be challenging for many leaders. If you haven't done the work of building the earlier foundational elements of mission, vision, and strategy, it's hard to know where to begin when it comes to organizing your team and also sheds light on why you tend to start with who first.

When you start with who, the mission of your organization is a slave to the preferences, strengths, and whims of your existing team. It doesn't illuminate what you need to accomplish the mission.

The goal of a well-designed organizational chart is for every role to support the strategy that achieves your mission.

When you start with what, you let the mission and strategy guide you. When you approach your org chart this way, you are ensuring alignment between your mission and the daily activities of your team.

The goal of a well-designed organizational chart is for every role to support the strategy that achieves your mission. To do this, you start with your strategy and work backward. While space doesn't allow me to cover every nuanced step of this process, here are a few key points to get you started:

Think functions, not specific people.
Pretend you have a clean slate and are hiring a completely new team. It's likely that in your current scenario your marketing manager is synonymous with Suzy who has done marketing for you for the last ten years. By having Suzy in mind, you will only think about the marketing role with

her strengths in mind. You want to remove personalities from this process to help you be more objective about what the organization needs to achieve the mission.

Based upon your strategy, determine what key functions are essential to your organization.

Most organizations will have some common key functions like Operations, which may include accounting, finance, IT, facilities, etc. But based upon the nature of your business and your strategic priorities, you may have a primary function of Content Writing while someone else may have a primary function of Donor Development or Fundraising. Determine the three to five high-level primary functions of your organization. These will serve as your highest-level leadership roles under your most senior leader.

Once you've determined these high-level primary functions, you can begin identifying the next tier of roles that report into these key functions.

As you build this, you're considering the needs and scale of your business. There is no right answer to the number of roles that should be on your org chart, but best practices related to your industry and internal benchmarks will serve as a helpful guide.

Continue the above process for as many layers of structure your organization requires.

For most small businesses and nonprofits, this is rarely more than four levels of organizational structure.

Create role responsibilities.

In addition to defining the roles, you'll want to create role responsibilities and expectations that will become the filters for helping you choose your who.

Once you've completed this process, you are sitting with a beautifully designed org chart that is aligned to your strategy.

Now the challenging work begins. But before we get there, I want to emphasize the importance of this ideal org chart. It's ideal, and we know that when we're talking about leading culture, nothing is ideal. This ideal structure, however, is your North Star. It is what you come back to every time you have changes in your staffing so you can continue to make decisions that best align with your strategy to achieve your mission.

THE WHO PROBLEM

With your ideal structure in hand, you're likely feeling pretty optimistic (as long as you've focused on what so far). You see the potential alignment. Some of the gaps in your current structure have been addressed in this design. Now you must wrestle with the reality of who you currently have on the team.

I want to take a minute and emphasize the importance of bringing your heart to this work. After an exercise of focusing on what you need to accomplish the mission, you might feel emboldened to release your current staff and start fresh. This is not what I'm advocating. I simply want you to start with the what and get a picture in your mind of the structure that best serves your strategy.

Now comes the hard part. This is why leading culture is an essential skill for every leader. Leading culture requires we live in the constant tension of what versus who. We are always balancing both priorities and making the best possible decisions that we can.

The *who* part of the org chart work is exciting. Remember how I told you that you're responsible for stewarding both the mission of your organization and the people who are a part of it? I deeply believe that an important part of culture is the stewardship of people in pursuit of a mission. The stewardship of people requires our willingness to be brutally honest about the needs of the organization (your ideal org chart) and the gifts and talents of your team.

Now your job is to look for matches. Again, I can't account for every nuance you will face but here are a few key points to keep in mind:

Don't jump to the obvious conclusions.
Just because Suzy has been your marketing director for the past ten years does not make her the obvious choice for the marketing director today. Review the role description and expectations you've defined and make an honest evaluation of her fit now.

Consider new possibilities.
If Suzy is not the best fit for the role she previously held, consider if there might be a better seat for her in the new structure. This is actually one of the most exciting things that often emerges in this work—by opening our mind to

different possibilities, we often find roles for people that we would have never previously considered.

Look for natural fits.
Continue working through each team member, looking for the natural fits. When you get stuck, consider any slight modifications that could be made without sacrificing alignment with your strategy and mission. Remember, your ideal org chart is your baseline. If you need to make adjustments, you are now making conscious choices as you are weighing the two priorities of your mission and your people.

Be honest about who doesn't fit.
You'll likely identify a person or two who simply doesn't fit. Maybe they held a legacy role that no longer supports your strategy. If you've sincerely tried to find a place for them but have been unable to, it's time to consider how to graciously move them on. (We'll say more about this process in chapter 8.)

Okay, now it's time to take a deep breath. This is big, important work! In fact, I can't emphasize adequately how key this process is to the health of your team.

Here's why . . .

EVERYONE HAS A PLACE

Every person on your team is asking if their role matters.

Purpose is more important than ever to your team. They want to be a part of meaningful work; whether it's subconscious or not, they are asking where they fit and why it matters. A well-designed organizational chart reflects how each player on your team contributes and emphasizes that every role is mission critical. This is incredibly powerful!

Without the clarity of an organizational structure that reflects every mission-critical role on the team, employees are left to create their own interpretations of the importance of their work and where they fit within the team.

One of the common criticisms I hear from leaders about bringing clarity to their organizational structure is that it feels too bureaucratic, or it emphasizes hierarchy. I understand the sentiment. Workplace culture today is much more democratic and collaborative. There is a cultural pushback against structures of power that diminish or demoralize others.

However, these concerns don't dismiss the need to bring clarity to how your team is organized. Lack of organization doesn't necessarily reduce power abuses; in some cases, it may give controlling leaders license to wield more power.

Our broader culture, especially in the West, conditions us to expect hierarchy. Every institution we're a part of, from schools to churches to government entities to sports teams to family units, has either a clear structure of power or at a minimum an understood structure of power. Whenever we engage a group of people working together, we are determining where we fit in the structure and quickly identifying who the leaders are.

When you provide clarity to the structure and establish how this structure serves the strategy that helps you achieve your mission, you are connecting the dots for every team member to understand why and how their role matters. It ties the organization's purpose to their purpose. In providing this clarity, you've reduced the frustration and confusion that exists when structures aren't clear, and you empower every team member to feel confident in the purpose of their work.

RESPONSIBILITIES AND EXPECTATIONS

The final step of your organizational structure is ensuring that not only is every role in the structure clear, but every role has clear responsibilities and expectations. This is another level of clarity that when not provided creates frustration for your team.

Role Profile

For each role on your org chart, you need a set of core responsibilities. You might call this a job description or a role profile, but whatever you call it, you want to make sure that it's clear, concise, and current.

- *Clear*—an employee can read the description and have a strong understanding of how they should be spending their time and energy.
- *Concise*—it doesn't need to be five pages long. In fact, a one-page description with clear bulleted responsibilities is typically plenty. You don't want to overwhelm; you want to empower.

- *Current*—make sure it's up to date. The role profile you wrote five years ago is likely no longer accurate. Keep role profiles current so that you and your employee have a clear sense of their responsibilities.

Performance Plans

Not only does your team need to understand their core responsibilities as defined in their role profile, but they also need to have clear goals that help them prioritize their work.

Performance plans are how you cascade organizational priorities to team member responsibilities. Think of it this way: The performance plan is like the magnifying glass that zooms in on the most important parts of their role profile in a given time period. Both tools work together to help team members give their best energy to the most important work.

While role profiles are more static (evaluated and updated with org chart changes), performance plans are time-bound documents. You could create performance plans for any duration of time, but I typically see them anywhere from quarterly to annually. Personally, I prefer writing performance plans in six-month increments to ensure we actively use them. Additionally, it simplifies the number of goals on the plan, making it more focused and less overwhelming. (We'll talk more about performance plans in chapter 8.)

"Wow! This was not what I expected," Alli shared as we were wrapping up the organizational clarity work. "I was really dreading this part. Org charts have always felt a little . . . I guess . . . heartless to me. I'm a people person and so I've always thought that structure was too stuffy and impersonal. Now I get it."

"Yeah," Sam chimed in. "This work we've done today is going to be a game changer for our team. I didn't realize how much I was holding back and not contributing at my best all because I lacked clarity. I feel so much more ener-gized about our work, and I really think the team will as well. I can't wait for us to share it with them!"

Steve had been sitting quietly for the last few minutes. Slowly he leaned forward and spoke up: "I've always thought that things like org charts, role descriptions, and perfor-mance plans were bureaucratic mumbo jumbo that only big corporations needed to make themselves feel important. I kind of prided myself on our organic way of working as a team, but I'm realizing that my laissez-faire attitude about this has actually hindered us. I haven't served the team well by undervaluing these tools that are so essential for clarity. I'm really sorry, you guys, and I'm committed to valuing this as we move forward."

The team had done really good work. They had wres-tled through some complexity in their org chart, but while there was a lot they were excited about implementing, they also had some hard decisions to make. A few legacy posi-tions needed to be changed and some role clarity meant conversations were needed to clarify responsibilities and expectations for a few team members.

A NOTE ABOUT IMPLEMENTATION

While I have emphasized the immense value of providing organizational clarity by way of your organizational chart, roles, responsibilities, and performance plans, I need to stress that how you lead through these changes is extraordinarily critical. You will need to define a thoughtful approach to rolling out organizational changes to your team. The scope of the changes you are making will determine the process.

Every situation will have nuances, so while I can't prescribe an exact process or formula, here are a few best practices to consider as you think through your communication plan:

Invite feedback.
Review the changes with your HR professional to get their insight and recommendations.

Consider the impact.
Put yourself in the shoes of each person on the team who will be impacted by the changes and consider what they need to know, when they need to know it, and how they would prefer to hear it.

Communicate respectfully.
Make sure you communicate to people in appropriate order. Consider who needs to know what information and create

a communication plan that respectfully communicates to people at the right time.

Don't rush this process.
While you're excited about the changes you've defined, how you lead through this will impact your culture. Org clarity work done haphazardly can actually be more detrimental to your culture. Be patient and persistent in your implementation.

FINAL THOUGHTS ON ORGANIZATIONAL CLARITY

Providing organizational clarity is an absolute game changer for your culture. So many teams struggle because leaders undervalue the fundamentals that provide clarity and build trust for their team.

When this foundation is secure, you've built trust by providing the essential things that employees need to feel confident in their role and what's required of them. With this understanding and the confidence it creates, they are now equipped to engage at more meaningful levels of contribution and ownership.

CULTURE TEAM
ACTION PLAN

↳ Using the following Clarity Check as a guide, evaluate the core elements of organizational clarity and determine where critical gaps are.

↳ Make a plan to address these gaps.

A note of caution: The work we've outlined in this chapter is extensive. Many of these pieces of organizational clarity can be very time-consuming depending on the amount of work necessary. As you discuss these core elements as a team, resist the urge to rush them. Be honest about the current state, and as a team define a plan to address them. Don't try to tackle all of them at once.

↳ Identify the category that you believe is creating the most confusion for your team and address that first. They do tend to have a cascading effect, so work them in this order if possible:
  • Vision
  • Strategy
  • Organizational Structure
  • Roles and Responsibilities
  • Performance Plans

CLARITY CHECK

	Yes	No
We have a vision statement.	☐	☐

If yes, how measurable and compelling is our vision statement? 1= not clear at all, 5 = very clear

1 2 3 4 5

We have a strategic plan to achieve our mission.	☐	☐

If yes, how clearly does every person on our team understand their part in achieving the strategy? 1= not clear at all, 5 = very clear

1 2 3 4 5

We have an organizational structure.	☐	☐

If yes, how strongly does our structure support your strategy? 1= not strong at all, 5 = very strong

1 2 3 4 5

Everyone on our team has clearly defined roles and responsibilities outlined in a role description.	☐	☐
Each team member has a performance plan with clear goals.	☐	☐

Go to culturemattersbook.com/resources for additional resources from this chapter.

PHASE 3

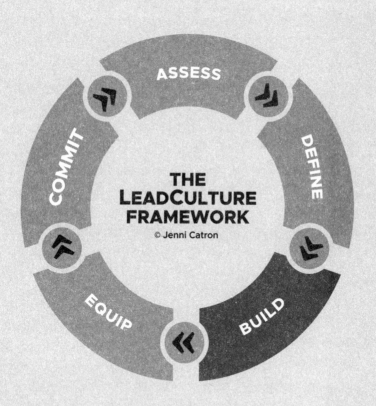

8

Creating the Rhythms
That Protect Your Culture

"Environment is the invisible hand that
shapes human behavior."

—James Clear[30]

"How are we going to implement all of this?" Steve's team asked with a mix of overwhelm and determination.

They had put in a lot of effort up to this point. As we worked through their organizational clarity, they realized how the vision had gotten lost in all the chaos; they discovered that all their roles had changed because of the strategy shifts they had made, and that not clarifying the org chart was causing tremendous confusion and frustration. Our work created clarity, but in fighting for that clarity, they now were more committed than ever to protecting it. Their question was, How?

CULTURE IS A SYSTEM

Culture is the system that fosters the values, beliefs, and behaviors of a group. If you're not designing the system, you will default to one—and likely an ineffective one. That may be the most important revelation you need in order to make your culture great.

The idea that culture needs a system is counterintuitive. Culture is about people, and as soon as we start talking about people and systems it conjures up feelings of corporate bureaucracy and heartless leadership. Remember when I said that clarity is the chief indicator of the health of a culture? Systems provide clarity, and as author and researcher Brené Brown has famously said, "Clear is kind." Building your people operating system is one of the kindest things you can do for your team. The system brings consistency to how you live out "who you are and how you work together to achieve your mission."

Culture is the system that fosters the values, beliefs, and behaviors of a group.

Lack of a system is why your team members are disengaged.

Lack of a system is why your values were an episodic exercise that didn't take root.

Lack of a system is why your hiring is ineffective.

EMPLOYEE JOURNEY GRID
VALUES X BEHAVIOR = CULTURE

RHYTHM	RITUAL / REMINDERS		
	What	Who	When
Interviewing & Hiring			
Onboarding			
Meetings & Communication Tools			
All Staff Meetings			
1:1 Meetings			
Annual Planning / Retreats			
Other Communication Tools			
Performance Plans & Reviews			
Performance Plans			
Performance Reviews			
Organizational Survey			
Training & Development			
Departures			
Other			

© Jenni Catron

Lack of a system is why you can't get momentum for your strategy.

Lack of a system is why there is no consistency in your communication.

Lack of a system is why there is confusion in roles and responsibilities.

Lack of a system is why you scramble to pull together an agenda for your staff meeting.

Now that you've done the work to assess your current culture and define what you aspire to, it's time to build the system that brings your ideal culture to life!

THE EMPLOYEE JOURNEY

The purpose behind this work is to effectively serve and support the people on your team. People are the point. We're not building a system for the system's sake; we're building a system to support the team. If we're not clear about the point of the system, the system will become the point and the bureaucracy you fear will become your reality.

For this reason, the system is built around the employee's experience with your organization. Every person on your team goes on a journey with your organization and there is a beginning and an end. For some, that journey may be a year or two; for others it may be decades. Regardless of tenure (although our intention is that the system increases the length of their journey), the question you must ask is, What kind of experience are you creating? Is it a haphazard and chaotic experience that leaves them exhausted, or is it a purposeful and exhilarating experience that brings out the best in them?

Employees are giving the best hours of their day to the work they do in your organization. Your goal is to make that time incredibly meaningful and valuable.

There are six stages to the employee journey:

1. Interviewing
2. Onboarding
3. Meeting Rhythms & Communication Tools
4. Performance Plans & Reviews
5. Training & Development
6. Departure

This list probably feels pretty benign to you—nothing revolutionary here, right? I suspect you have some systems for most of these stages, but I want you to consider whether you've ever thought of these stages as a means to build culture. If you're like most leaders, you've seen them more as compliance practices and less about culture building. I want you to see these stages as essential to your culture operating system.

Each of these stages needs to be infused with your defined and preferred culture. At each stage you're clarifying "who you are and how you work together to achieve your mission."

Stage 1: Interviewing

Every person on your team is contributing to your culture, positively or negatively. Therefore, how you interview and who you hire has a tremendous effect on your culture.

One thing that I see leaders do all too frequently is rush hiring decisions out of desperation. You have an open position, you get connected to somebody who may be a great fit, and you throw them into the role because you don't really have a process for vetting them.

And then suddenly, you realize they are not a great fit. This person is not aligned with your culture, or they don't actually have the skills for the job. Now you've made a long-term commitment to someone with whom you had a short introduction.

When we make poor hiring decisions, we leave ourselves with a much more challenging management issue. A poor hiring decision is more costly and more painful than a slow hiring decision.

A common practice in hiring is to follow the three Cs: character, chemistry, and competence. I believe there is a fourth, equally critical *C* to consider—you guessed it: culture.

Character—We want people of integrity.

Chemistry—We want people we enjoy working with.

Competence—We want people who know how to do the work, or at a minimum have the ability to learn it.

Culture—We want people who value who we are and how we work together.

In the hiring process, culture is often overlooked or assumed. In fact, we often mistake chemistry for culture. You connected well with the candidate, and you assume they'll be a good culture fit. Someone could be enjoyable to have dinner with but may not share your values and beliefs. That's the distinction in culture. In fact, someone could actually be a great culture fit and not be someone you want to hang out with in your free time. The discipline is in recognizing that the culture fit is a better hire than the chemistry fit. Of course, the preference is that they meet the criteria for all four Cs.

When you're interviewing for culture, you're interviewing for alignment with the values, beliefs, and behaviors you've defined—the values that are critical to who you are and how you work together. You need to make sure that in your interviewing process, you are interviewing for culture alignment, not just character, chemistry, and competence.

"Oof! We're terrible at this," Elizabeth confessed. "We love hiring friends or friends of friends, but too often once they join the team, we realize there were some things we didn't see ahead of time. Because they are friends it's even harder to have the discussion of why they're not a fit."

"I agree," Steve chimed in. "And I need to take responsibility for this. I think I've wanted to keep us feeling like a family, so I've overemphasized chemistry fit to the detriment of the culture."

Nearly every head in the room nodded in agreement. What Steve acknowledged is a common issue for many leaders, especially founding leaders. I could sense in that moment that Steve was beginning to see just how much influence he had in shaping the culture and how his renegade style had been hindering them.

CULTURE TEAM
ACTION PLAN

↳ In partnership with your HR professional, review your current interview process. If you don't currently have a process, make a plan to build one.

↳ Consider where and how you can interview for values alignment.

- Add interview questions that help you get a sense of the candidate's core personal values.
- Add interview questions in which you're asking the candidate to describe how they would respond to a scenario. Evaluate if their responses are aligned with your values.

Stage 2: Onboarding

Onboarding is the single greatest opportunity you have to equip a new employee to quickly learn who you are and how you work together as a team.

While selecting team members is critical, how you onboard them will have significant impact on your culture, for good or bad, both for the team and the new employee. You want to be sure you set them up to be in alignment. New team members typically don't join your team with the intent of negatively impacting your culture. They are eager to be a part; however, they are bringing their previous cultural experience to your organization. Without intentional education about your culture, they may unintentionally bring some habits and behaviors that are out of alignment with your defined culture.

Both you and the new employee are eager for them to fit in. You're excited for them to be a part of the team and, frankly, you're relieved you've filled the role that was vacant. Because of this eagerness and well-intentioned belief in the new employee, you will be tempted to shortchange the onboarding process because "they get us." You've found a great candidate that you believe in and are confident they understand who you are, and you figure they'll catch what they need to know.

If your culture is incredibly clear at all levels of the organization and if you can say with great confidence that every team member is fully aligned with your culture, then you may be able to leave their culture onboarding to chance. But if you're like most organizations, culture drift is pervasive. It's easy for an individual or department to get slightly off course. My encouragement to you is, don't leave it to chance. To protect your culture, you want to give every new team member the courtesy of fully understanding how you define who you are and how you work together to achieve your mission. They deserve the best shot at positively contributing to the health of your team.

"I love the idea of creating a plan for onboarding new employees to our culture!" exclaimed Alli. "I so want new team members to feel a part of what we're doing, and I can't help but feel bad if we're talking about something in a meeting and a new person has no idea about the backstory. I'd happily volunteer to help facilitate this part of the onboarding once we build our plan."

There are two key elements of your culture onboarding plan:

1. Your employee handbook
2. Values training

Your employee handbook
I realize that your employee handbook is not the most excit-ing resource in your leadership toolkit, but I believe that is because we've resorted to seeing it as a necessary evil rather than seeing it as a valuable resource to serve your team. I challenge you to change your perspective on the impor-tance of this document. This is not just a resource to satisfy HR professionals; this is a document that can capture in writing the heart and spirit of your organization.

Here are some specific things to consider in your employee handbook:

Align the language—Rewrite the language in a tone that reflects who you are. Too many times I see employee handbooks (and other process documents) written in a completely different style from the culture of the organi-zation. It's no wonder employees don't pay any attention to these documents. They don't reflect who you are and how you work together. Your written documentation either aligns with your culture or it doesn't.

Incorporate your values—As you read the employee handbook, is there any part of it that feels in conflict with your values? For example, does the tone of the document convey skepticism or lack of trust (this usually shows up in legal language), which feels incongruent with your value of "believing the best" of one another? Work with your HR professional to say the important compliance parts of your employee handbook in a way that is also consistent with your values. Remember, your values become the filter for everything you do.

Include your values grid—Make sure there is a section of your employee handbook that includes your values grid. This usually goes hand in hand with your mission and vision information.

Your employee handbook is your team's written reference for how to succeed in your organization. Be sure it's a tool that truly reflects who you aspire to be.

Values Training

Remember all the work you did to define and create your values grid? There are stories and insights that are impossible to capture in your values grid, and it's a disservice to your new employees if they don't hear these legends and history. If you're not careful, your values grid can become insider language privy only to the few who helped create it. To combat this, you need a process for ensuring that every team member is caught up on these insider anecdotes that bring so much understanding to how your culture was shaped and formed.

In one organization I led, we created a class we called Culture Shock that each new team member was enrolled in. It was a once-a-month lunch with an executive team member who shared one of the organizational values, shared the story behind the value, and taught the beliefs and behaviors that supported the value. They shared examples and talked about the ways the team lives the values day to day. In addition to being a great way to communicate the values, having executive team members rotate through the sessions helped new team members get to know their most senior leaders and hear those leaders express the importance of the values.

CULTURE TEAM
ACTION PLAN

↳ Review and rewrite your employee handbook to reflect the personality of your culture. When you defined your culture, a personality emerged. Are you a fun and energetic team? Are you a professional and detailed team? (Reference the Who We Are statement you created in chapter 4.) There is no right or wrong answer; it's about understanding who you are and making sure your written document reflects your style.

↳ Consider how to integrate new team members into your values. Get creative and have some fun with this.

↳ Create a plan for ensuring that every new team member will go through your values alignment process.

Stage 3: Meeting Rhythms & Communication Tools

Your culture operating system will be most successful when it's integrated into the rhythms that are already established within your organization. Oftentimes Culture Teams assume they need to create all new meetings and rhythms for culture. In your initial enthusiasm, you'll be tempted to do this, but I strongly recommend you consider your current structure and add your culture work into those existing rhythms. Your current meeting structure can be a consistent place to reinforce your culture.

One of the most important principles to remember about culture change is that it requires patience and persistence.

Patience + Persistence = Culture Change

Meetings are an existing avenue to persistently communicate, celebrate, and reinforce your values, beliefs, and behaviors. Let's look at some of your different meeting types and some ideas and examples for how to reinforce your culture in these environments.

All-staff meeting

As a leader, time with your entire staff is valuable vision-casting time. This is your opportunity to make sure your greatest priorities are communicated and your strongest values are reinforced. If your all-staff meeting feels like a waste of time or has been a bureaucratic agenda of details, you first need to re-envision this meeting. Tally up the cost of every employee being paid to attend this meeting and you'll discover this is your most expensive meeting. Therefore, it should be your most valuable meeting to ensure alignment in all areas and particularly in culture. You have the undivided attention of your staff all at the same time. This meeting is your culture juggernaut. Use it that way.

Ideas on how to integrate culture into your all-staff meeting:

- Highlight a value in each meeting and celebrate stories of team members who have demonstrated that value.
- Create an opportunity for team members to call out others who they've seen demonstrating a value.
- Celebrate birthdays and work anniversaries of your team each month.

Here's an example:

One organization I worked with does Mile Marker celebrations for their staff who have hit work anniversaries. They create roadside mile marker signs for team members at their 1, 3, 5, 10+ anniversaries, and team members proudly display them in their offices.

One word of caution: Keep these ideas fresh and make sure they're facilitated by someone who brings good energy and enthusiasm. The danger of rhythms is that they can become mundane. This work is too important to let it become boring. Your culture efforts will become a negative if the team senses you're just going through the motions because you think you're supposed to. If you believe that your team is worth it and that protecting your culture is imperative to achieving your mission, be sure you're giving it your best energy.

One-on-one meeting
How your employees experience your culture is most acutely felt by their interactions with their manager. One-on-one meetings between employees and their manager are an important place for conversations around alignment with values to occur. If a team member is struggling with embodying a value, this is the place for coaching conversations to happen. If an employee experiences inconsistencies in the culture, this is a place for them to voice observations and to ask questions. Conversations around culture should be as common here as conversations around performance and goals.

Ideas for one-on-one meetings:

- As a manager, notice when your team members are living out an organizational value and thank them for it in your one-on-one time. (You may also do a shout-out in all-staff meetings but private thanks are also very valuable, sometimes more valuable depending on personality.)
- Create conversation-starter questions based upon your values and provide them to your managers for regular discussions in their one-on-one meetings.

Other communication tools

What additional tools do you have for communicating to your entire staff? Are there resources you need to create that help you communicate your most important values on a regular basis?

Here are some examples to spark ideas:

- If you have a weekly staff newsletter, add a section that highlights a value of the week or shares a story of a team member living out a value.

- If you use a team communication app like Teams or Slack, add a channel for #values or #atourbest and encourage staff to share stories of other team members living out your values.

- Hashtag your values in emails to one another. "Hey everyone, just a note to let you know that I'll be out of the office Tues–Thur for a conference. #leadyourselfwell"

- If you use a people development software, add a value of the week to your home page for your team to see and reflect on.

"Are we really sure all of this is necessary?" Sam asked. "It just feels like a lot of work. Surely now that we've defined our values, we can share those with the team and get back to business. This seems like a lot of effort, and you all know how busy we are."

I noticed a few team members considering Sam's question but sensed they were conflicted and unsure of whether to speak up. "What do the rest of you think?" I prompted.

"Sam's not wrong . . . at least about how busy we all are," Alex added. "I can see the value of the consistency, and the patience and persistence thing makes a lot of sense. It's just a little overwhelming to think about how to implement it all."

I was happy to see the team wrestling with this. They needed to feel the scope of it and begin to grapple with their commitment to it. Their commitment was going to be key to this working for their organization.

"I think you both raise some important points, and I would be a little concerned if you all weren't feeling this way. This is a lot of work, and it is a big commitment. The question you have to address is whether the stewardship of your team is important enough to your mission to make this commitment. Let's do this . . . keep wrestling with those questions as I continue to share the rest of the framework and then we'll have an opportunity at the end to decide how you want to proceed."

CULTURE TEAM
ACTION PLAN

↳ Review your meeting rhythms and brainstorm the best way to reinforce your values consistently.

↳ Work with the person who leads your all-staff meeting and present ideas for reinforcing culture and values regularly in this meeting.

↳ Partner with HR to make a plan for equipping your people managers to incorporate culture conversations in their one-on-one meetings with employees.

↳ Review your other communication tools and make a plan for infusing culture into those tools.

Stage 4: Performance Plans & Reviews

For most teams, performance plans and reviews are looked upon with dread. They feel pejorative and bureaucratic. Both employee and manager are looking for the quickest way through the process to be able to satisfy HR with the right documentation. I think it's safe to say that most of the time, performance plans and reviews are a negative in your organizational culture.

I want to challenge you to flip this perception. Performance plans and reviews could foster some of the most meaningful conversations for your team. Performance plans provide guidance for growth and development, and performance reviews are intentional conversations by which you as a manager can give meaningful feedback and helpful coaching.

First, let's define these terms and highlight their distinctions.

Performance plan

A performance plan is a written plan for each employee that defines the goals they need to achieve to succeed in their role. The duration of your plan should be defined—I recommend either six-month or twelve-month plans. Less than six months is typically too short, and more than twelve months is too long. You want to follow a duration that is reasonable for you to consistently commit to.

My preferred performance plan has three categories of goals:

1. Role-specific goals: These are performance-based goals directly related to the employee's role responsibilities.
2. Development goals: These are development-based goals outlining ways the employee can grow in their skills and their future aspirations.
3. Values goals: These are goals related to living into your organizational values.

The number of goals on the plan and each category may vary based upon priorities, but I typically use the following formula to serve as a guide:

-   Three or four role-specific goals that can be tied (directly or indirectly) to the organization's goals for this same time period.
-   One or two development goals specifically for this team member that positions them to continue to grow in the skills necessary to succeed in their role. Typically, these goals are related to "soft" skills and/or ongoing training for their area of specialty.
-   One values goal related to how this team member can align with your organizational values. While all your values are important for the employee to embody, you're typically selecting one value that

either the employee has more trouble living into or a value that will be very important to supporting their other goals in this season.

This will result in five to seven goals for the duration of the plan. While that may not sound like enough, the intention is for these to be the greatest areas of focus for this team member. The performance plan is not designed to capture every responsibility an employee has (their role profile does that). This is meant to highlight their most important contribution in this season. When they feel torn between competing priorities, the performance plan provides focus.

The following are the elements of a good performance plan:

It must align with organizational strategy—Begin with an understanding of the overall organizational strategic plan and goals for the predetermined duration of time (semiannually or annually).

It should be written by the employee—Employees should write their performance plan and then refine the plan with their manager's input. This is important for two reasons:

1. The employee is closer to the needs and priorities, so they'll typically surface better goals.
2. They'll take greater ownership of a plan they've written.

The goals should be clear and achievable—Tools like SMART goals are helpful here. You should be able to answer a clear yes or no to whether the goal was achieved when you conduct the performance review.

Performance review

The performance review is simply the process for ensuring you follow up on the plan that was created. The performance review should happen in two parts:

Ongoing review and discussion of the performance plan in your one-on-one meetings—These regular conversations provide support and coaching to enable the employee to succeed in their goals. Providing real-time feedback helps them course correct and build confidence in their contribution to the team and therefore empowers them to contribute to the culture in a meaningful way. The reverse is also true. Without regular feedback they may disengage or drift out of alignment.

An intentional performance review session—This is your official review discussion where you confirm whether they completed the goals that they had set to achieve for the predetermined time frame. Nothing in this meeting should come as a surprise if you've been having regular ongoing discussions of their plan. This is simply the discussion to wrap up the existing plan (supported with written documentation) and to begin writing the plan for the next season.

In addition to reviewing the written performance plan, your organization may choose to include additional elements as part of the performance review process. For example, I would recommend evaluating all employees on how they model all your values, not just the one that was a part of their plan. Whatever you decide is a part of your review process needs to be communicated well to employees ahead of time so that they know what to expect from the process.

The obvious way that culture is infused in performance plans and reviews is by including values as a part of the process. The more subtle way that culture is impacted is by the clarity the process provides. By defining clear goals and reviewing them regularly, you are building trust with your employees. They understand what is expected of them and can be confident the process will create the right avenues for feedback and support.

CULTURE TEAM
ACTION PLAN

↳ Review your current system for performance plans and reviews, and determine what adjustments need to be made to better support your culture.

↳ Work with your HR team to implement changes.

Organizational survey

In addition to reviewing individual team members, you also want to have a regular rhythm of reviewing the organization. The feedback needs to go both ways. This is where the culture survey that you instigated in the assessment phase of the process shows up in your ongoing organizational rhythms. As previously noted, you can choose the frequency of surveying your team, but I recommend at least once a year.

An important part of the survey process is that you maintain a commitment to evaluating the feedback and taking action on what you're hearing from staff. The annual survey of your team will provide an important data point for how you're doing in realizing the culture you aspire to. This will be one of the most important tools for your ongoing assessment of the health of your culture.

CULTURE TEAM ACTION PLAN

↳ Determine the frequency of your ongoing survey.
↳ Create questions around your values for part two of your survey.
↳ Define a process for analyzing survey results and taking action each year (we'll talk more about this in chapter 11).

Stage 5: Training & Development

As you consider the existing rhythms within your organization, what methods for training and development exist formally or informally? Ongoing training and development is an essential and healthy part of the employee journey. The speed of change is greater than ever, and keeping employees well equipped with the tools they need to succeed (remember level 1 of the hierarchy) is an important part of a healthy culture. Employees feel valued and supported when training and development are a consistent part of your organizational rhythms.

CULTURE TEAM
ACTION PLAN

↳ Discuss your current plan for training and development. How does it reinforce the culture you aspire to?

↳ What tweaks could you make to your current system to be sure your values are reinforced?

If you do not have a consistent system for training and development, here are some questions to help you define what you need to create:

↳ What consistent behaviors of your team are not serving your culture well? Do you have a habit of poor communication, poor time management, or lack of collaboration (just to name a few)? These behaviors don't have to be directly tied to a value, but you know they affect your culture in a negative way.

↳ Review the behaviors that you defined for each value on your values grid. Which of these behaviors does your team need training for?

↳ Assemble your list of training needs. Identify a point person who can take ownership of this project and then build a one-to-two-year plan for regularly training to address these topics.

In chapter 10 on leadership, I outline more ideas and recommendations for training your leaders to support your culture.

Note for the point person: You don't need to be the expert or trainer for these topics. You simply need to be passionate about equipping your team, administratively committed to organizing a plan for training, prepared to communicate that plan to staff, and willing to facilitate. There are numerous resources you can access to do the actual training so that you can focus on facilitating. Resources may include books, online videos and/or courses, webinars, online conferences, podcasts, etc.

Stage 6: Departure

One of the often-overlooked stages of the employee journey that has significant impact on your culture is the departure of team members. Departures are unsettling, especially if the circumstances surrounding someone's leaving are unclear.

When beloved team members depart for a good reason (moving, promotion, new opportunity, staying home with their family, retirement, etc.), team members are sad because they know they are losing someone who contributed positively to the culture. It's a loss and no matter how happy we are for them, we grieve.

In these moments, the team is watching to make sure their leaders are appropriately honoring the departing individual. If you act in any way that feels dismissive, like you've "moved on," or that isn't aligned with the values you profess, it will break trust.

When team members depart for performance, character, or culture misalignment, these departures can be tricky. Typically, the nature of these departures is such that it is not appropriate for all staff to know all the details. This creates a potential breach of trust. Team members lack clarity around the departure and therefore will fill in the gaps with stories they hear from others and/or stories they tell themselves about what leaders here do.

If your leadership team consistently demonstrates alignment with values in their day-to-day operations, your team is more likely to default to assuming the best in these scenarios where details are not appropriate. This is where consistency and clarity breed trust over time and pay off in providing you the benefit of the doubt when you need it. When leaders are consistent in cultural behaviors, team members are confident to trust in difficult moments. Ultimately, they are trusting the consistency of your character and can count on you making these decisions congruent with your values and beliefs as a team.

Remember, as much as team members are mourning the departure of a colleague, the bigger concern on their mind is, "What does this mean for me?" With any departure, there is bound to be a shifting of responsibilities to cover the loss until the position is refilled and a new person is fully trained. It impacts other team members when someone departs, and they immediately feel that burden. In circumstances where the departure is more tenuous and details are sparse, team members may fear for their own future. They may wonder if layoffs are on the horizon or if they are performing up to expectations. Fear and doubt creep in during times of uncertainty. Leaders need to be aware of these fears and be prepared to address them.

When leaders are consistent in cultural behaviors, team members are confident to trust in difficult moments.

Two key elements for healthy departures:

1. Consistency
   For departures instigated by the organization, a clear and consistent process needs to be in place. Team members need to be assured there is a process and that the decision to release an employee is not a hasty one.

2. Communication
   Communication is key for every departure. It's important to have a plan for what you communicate and how you communicate. Determine ahead of time what your communication process is for both employee-instigated departures and organization-instigated departures.

A key part of leading culture is being willing to understand and empathize with what team members will be feeling in key moments. Departures drum up lots of feelings. Culture leaders will be wise to anticipate them.

"I'm just beginning to realize how much we've expected the staff to fill communication voids with positive intent. We've had so much turnover the last few years for a variety of reasons, and I've expected everyone to believe the best in how we're handling it. I didn't put myself in their shoes to realize how much anxiety this has caused," Steve shared, head down, slumped forward in his chair.

Elizabeth added, "Yeah, I think we're so close to all the information and we know our intention as leaders, so we assume everyone else gets that. I think we've been unintentionally expecting a lot from our team."

"I see two key issues," Tim spoke up. "First is consistency. We've been making excuses for postponing performance reviews and deferring training and development. Selfishly this was in large part to how busy I've been. I didn't account for the uncertainty this could create. Second is communication. We haven't communicated why we've stopped doing some of these things and then more critically, we have not had consistent process or communication around all the staff departures. We've just expected that everyone understands and, like you said, Steve, we've expected them to give us the benefit of the doubt."

Steve's team was clearly seeing the value of the consistency of rhythms and were more emboldened to build their employee journey grid and, more importantly, commit to being consistent with it.

CULTURE TEAM
ACTION PLAN

↳ Brainstorm how your values need to guide you when team members depart.

↳ Determine what core communication is necessary for every departure and work with HR to put a process in place to ensure consistency in communication.

↳ Work with HR to create a consistent process for how separation decisions are made when the organization is instigating the separation.

Your employee journey grid is a key resource in developing the rhythms that reinforce your culture on a day-to-day basis. Building this plan and committing to its implementation is a core part of your LeadCulture work.

CLARITY CHECK

	Yes	No
Our interview process is clear and consistent.	☐	☐
We have an onboarding plan that ensures culture alignment.	☐	☐
Our meeting rhythms positively contribute to our culture.	☐	☐
We have a consistent process for writing performance plans.	☐	☐
We have a consistent process for facilitating performance reviews.	☐	☐
We provide consistent training and leadership development for all team members.	☐	☐
We have a clear and consistent process for departing employees.	☐	☐

Go to culturemattersbook.com/resources for additional resources from this chapter.

PHASE 4

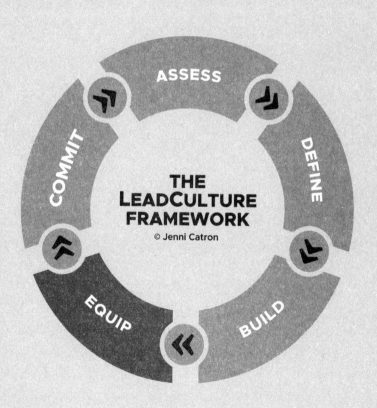

9

Equipping Your Team

> "By constantly reinforcing the values of the culture, companies can attract and retain individuals who value and thrive in that culture."
>
> —**Robert Spector**[31]

As we finished the first draft of their employee journey grid, Steve's team were beginning to get excited. As they had expressed, they were nervous about how to implement it all, but for the first time they felt like they could see a pathway for consistency in their culture. Like many other organizations, they had tried to do culture work here or there, but it typically felt like a rah-rah moment that was meaningful in the immediate but had little lasting impact.

They now understood the system they needed to create, and they had a first draft in hand.

As we were wrapping up that discussion and celebrating our work, Alli chimed in with a question: "I'm a little nervous to say this because I don't want to throw a wet blanket on all the good work we've done so far, but what about the rest of the staff? How do we catch them up on all this work we've done? It seems like we could create a divide in our culture quickly if we don't find a way to bring them up to speed."

I couldn't have been more proud of Alli in that moment! First, she brought up what would have historically been an uncomfortable question with much more ease. They were all feeling safer in bringing up unpleasant ideas and were continuing to model the culture they aspired to—one of thoughtful evaluation and respectful debate. Second, Alli was thinking on behalf of the entire staff. In the past everyone typically watched out for themselves or their immediate team and didn't give much concern to how decisions or actions impacted the rest of the staff. The question she posed was exactly the right one and was the next part of our process.

MOVING BEYOND THEORY

If you're still reading this, I'm insanely proud of you. You have done some enormously important culture-shaping work that has the potential to influence your organization for years to come. Now it's time to put this work into action. One of the most frustrating things you could do for you and your team is to have done all this work of defining an amazing culture plan and then leave it to collect dust on the proverbial shelf. I've had countless conversations with leaders who have done similar work and hired expensive consultants to no avail. When they ask me what will be different with the LeadCulture Framework, I tell them, "Nothing, unless you're willing to do the patient and persistent work of implementation."

You've done too much work to stop now—and here's the best part: this is when it starts to get really fun! You're moving beyond theory and ideas and putting your work into practice.

In this section, we're going to cover:

- Building your playbook and tools
- Onboarding your existing team
- The culture engagement funnel
- Critical skills you need to keep leading culture

BUILDING YOUR PLAYBOOK AND TOOLS

Before you roll this out to the entire team, you need to create the resources that reflect your work. You need to create the work product. Everything you've defined needs to be captured just like any other essential process in your organization should be documented in order to produce consistent results. Additionally, documentation becomes your curriculum for teaching culture. Without this written material you resort to culture simply being caught and you will not move the culture from caught to taught.

Create your playbook.

Great teams live and die by the playbook. I can't help but picture NFL coaches on the sidelines with their laminated colorful card of all the plays or the cheat sheet on a quarterback's wrist, which are shorthand versions of their playbook. Without the playbook guiding them, it would be chaos. The same is true for you and your team. You need to be operating from the same playbook.

Create visual assets.

Visuals create connections and associations that enable us to process and remember information better. Engage your visual artists and graphic designers to bring your values to life. Add icons or graphics that reflect your values. Use interesting text and design layout to take your values from grid form to something that is interesting and engaging.

These visual assets will be necessary for presentations and other resources that you'll create to onboard current and future team members.

ONBOARDING YOUR EXISTING TEAM

Your Culture Team is inspired and excited. You've done good work. You have clarified who you are and how you work together. With your values now defined and your employee journey grid built, it's imperative that you bring the rest of the team into the process.

There are many ways to do this, and I'm going to share some different ideas and suggestions to get you started. But here is a question I want you to wrestle with: If you were a staff person who was not on the Culture Team, what would it take for you to get excited about this plan and own it as if you were one of the original Culture Team members?

Your communication of the culture plan to the rest of the team is one of your first opportunities for everyone to begin to experience the culture you aspire to. If you've historically done a poor job of communicating new information to your team but this is a high value in your ideal culture, make sure your rollout plan is thoroughly communicated. If in the past your meetings were boring but your goal is to make meetings inspiring and engaging, here is your opportunity for your team to experience something different.

In our effort to truly create a culture operating system, the system begins by inviting all staff into the work. Your rollout plan will be equal parts the information you need to communicate and creating an experience that reflects who you aspire to be. Your rollout to the staff should not be an afterthought. It's the kickoff to the new culture you are creating!

CULTURE TEAM ACTION PLAN

↳ Review what you need to communicate. Be sure you've edited and finalized all the documents in your LeadCulture Framework and have assembled the first draft of your culture playbook.

↳ Brainstorm ways to roll this out to staff in a fun and engaging way. (If a talking head is scrolling

through a slide deck, you stand to hurt your culture more than help it.)

↳ Consider the pace of how you'll roll it out. I recommend a multiphased approach.

- Initial session: Explain why you did this work,
  who was chosen to be a part to it, and why this
  group was chosen. (Anticipate the questions
  you would ask if you were hearing it for the first
  time and seek to address them.) In this session,
  give them the overview of the process and why
  you're excited about it. Give them the plan for
  the rest of the rollout.

- Follow-up sessions: Share the values grid and
  why values are the anchor to your culture. Provide a high-level overview of your set of values.
  Give context for how you arrived at these values, talk about the debates you had, and explain
  why you ultimately landed on these core values.

- Over a series of meetings, walk through each
  value, providing detail for the value itself, the
  belief behind that value, the behaviors that
  reflect it, the language for it, and the stories
  that support it.

↳ Create tangible resources to keep the values visible for everyone. Repetition is the key to remembrance. Remember that the rest of the staff have
not had the benefit of all the time that the Culture
Team has spent in this work. They will feel like
they are drinking from a fire hose. It will be a lot of

information to absorb, and visible reminders will be helpful to reinforce the values that reflect the new culture you aspire to. Some ideas to consider:

- Small tchotchkes like a stress cube with the values listed
- Screensaver graphics for their computers
- T-shirts with the values (typically very fun with just the sticky statement)
- Posters to frame for office common areas

Here's a bonus idea: Cover one value per meeting in your staff meetings. Have a different Culture Team member present a value each meeting so that different voices from the Culture Team are sharing. Make it fun and memorable. Brainstorm a creative element or theme to make the meeting interesting.

Repetition is the key to remembrance.

Examples of how to do this: A preschool staff rented out an ice cream shop for a private event one afternoon to treat their team to a fun and festive day off-site to share their values. The Culture Team presented their values in pairs, and for a fun and memorable twist, they chose a familiar pop song that fit the theme of their value and lip-synced it.

One large multi-site church created a Values Roadshow where the Culture Team divided up in pairs to spend ninety minutes with each campus team and department within the organization. They curated an experience that included some fun activities around the values, discussion, and time for questions and answers. For a large staff, this created a much more intimate way to share the culture plan in an environment that made it feasible for everyone to ask questions.

"I'm so excited about this part!" Alli could hardly contain her enthusiasm. "I'm so eager for the staff to hear about this work. I think they are going to love it."

"I don't know . . ." Sam said a little hesitantly. "I think once they've had time to really understand it, they will get excited about it, but I think if we're not careful this could be like when we rolled out the new people development software last year. We talked such a big game about how amazing it was and then we didn't consistently talk about it or effectively train everybody. Now we all groan when someone brings it up. We really need to be purposeful about how we roll this out and, like Jenni has told us so many times, we'll need to be patient and persistent in our communication."

"Yeah, you're right, Sam," Alli conceded. "I just see so much potential and I'm really committed to doing this right."

THE CULTURE ENGAGEMENT FUNNEL

Up to this point I've preached the importance of culture moving from caught to taught. The power of this work is that once you've engaged the process, culture moves from caught to taught and then to caught again. As every team member learns and experiences the culture, they then begin to embody it and also start teaching it. The truth is that employees are always "catching" culture by observing how others in the organization do things. If you haven't first taught your ideal culture, they're not going to catch the right things. But once an organization has clarity on their culture and teaches it consistently, new team members are learning the culture both by teaching and catching.

The culture engagement funnel, found on the next page, is a simple graphic that demonstrates what is happening. On the left side is what leaders and the Culture Team are doing. On the right side is what employees are doing. Notice that at the midway point, a handoff occurs. Employees begin joining the leaders and the Culture Team in embodying and teaching the culture. At this point, your aspirational culture is starting to be actualized. The flywheel effect of every person throughout the organization embodying and teaching who you are and how you work together is producing the culture you hope for.

From the top of the funnel working down:

1. Leaders are defining the aspirational culture. Employees are listening.
2. Leaders are communicating how we'll work together through the lens of the values grid. Employees are learning.
3. Leaders are modeling the culture by living into the rhythms defined in the employee journey grid. Employees are now experiencing the culture.

4.   Employees are embodying the culture and leaders are supporting them through coaching.

5.   Employees are teaching the culture and leaders are celebrating them.

This tool is a great way to monitor engagement with your team. If employees aren't moving down the funnel, you may need to reevaluate how you're defining and communicating. Do you need to make some adjustments? What needs to be more clearly defined and communicated?

Also to note, you'll have employees at all levels within the funnel. New employees will be at the top. Long-tenured employees should be at the bottom.

CULTURE ENGAGEMENT FUNNEL

Leaders Define - Employees Listen

Leaders Communicate - Employees Learn

Leaders Model - Employees Experience

Leaders Support - Employees Embody

Leaders Celebrate - Employees Teach

© Jenni Catron

CRITICAL SKILLS YOU NEED TO KEEP LEADING THE CULTURE

If you only took away one concept from this book, I would implore you to recognize that culture work is ongoing work and needs your constant attention. If you work through the LeadCulture Framework and then hope your culture will magically be better without continued commitment, you will be sorely disappointed. Culture is building or eroding every day and it needs constant nurturing. The good news is that by engaging this process, you've done the heavy lifting. Now you need to patiently and persistently keep working the plan. That's the point of an operating system; it's designed to become a rhythmic part of how you work on a day-to-day basis. It's not a project. It's your way of working.

Culture work is ongoing work and needs your constant attention.

I've used these two words—*patience* and *persistence*—frequently throughout the process, but let's look at them a little more closely.

Patience and persistence

The reason so many cultures stay stuck is because leaders are unwillingly to patiently and persistently implement their operating system and give it time to produce change. At the heart of culture change is behavior change. Your team

has developed behaviors for how they work together—
some good and some not so good. By clarifying your aspirational culture you've defined a new target that inevitably
requires changes in everyone's behavior (including yours),
and behavior change takes time. Your culture didn't break
overnight, and it won't be fixed overnight. I realize that
statement might be more extreme than your situation, but
you get the sentiment. We're asking our team to change the
familiar—the behaviors that are likely serving them well
right now, or at least behaviors that keep the peace. Culture
work often gets messier before it gets better. In your effort
to behave differently you're going to do it awkwardly. This
is where patience and persistence come into play.

Patience: You're not unfamiliar with this word, although
most leaders don't like it. By definition, *patient* means "not
hasty . . . steadfast."[32]

Persistence: This is a word you might be a bit more
comfortable with. By definition, to persist means "to go on
resolutely or stubbornly in spite of opposition."[33]

You could also say you need to be steadfast and stubborn.
I don't care which two words you like better; what I care
about is that you recognize that these attributes are essential
to seeing your desired goal come to fruition. I need you to
commit to it for the sake of you, your team, and the hope
you've created by engaging this project so far. It will actually
be worse on your culture if you start this project with gusto
and then fail to follow through with patience and persistence.

What exactly do I mean by this? Here are a few scenarios that might come up that will require you to patiently
and persistently reinforce your culture plan:

- You'll be tempted to skip a values review in a staff meeting because of a more urgent issue.
- A really talented team member continues to violate a core value and you avoid addressing it.
- You're busy with a big project and you are tempted to cancel your staff outing.
- You urgently need to fill a critical open position and want to forego your hiring process because you found a "great" candidate.

I'm willing to bet that as you begin living into your culture operating plan, it will feel like everything is conspiring against you. This is the resistance inevitable in meaningful work. Don't be discouraged by it. Expect it and commit to the mantra "patience and persistence."

Change management

Essentially what I'm trying to convey to you is the importance of understanding and embracing change management. Leading others through change requires intentional commitment. You're leading others through change at a pace they can stand. Too much too fast and they resist. Too slow and they lose hope.

I was recently working with a construction company in the northeast to help them define and implement their culture operating system. In one of our monthly meetings, they expressed that the rest of the staff were eager to start talking about what we were going to do to change the culture. We had been in the assessment phase doing careful work to really hear and assess the current culture dynamic. When I heard their hunger to move to action, I knew they were ready for the next step of change.

Change management is the ability to read, discern, and guide a team to a new outcome. This skill is essential in effectively changing your organizational culture. Some leaders are naturally wired with a bit more intuition to discern how to pace change in a way that creates buy-in. These leaders feel their way through change and are typically quite successful. The problem with this approach is that because they are going with their gut, they don't know how to teach others to do it. Change management is a skill you can learn and frankly need to learn to be an effective leader.

5 Steps for Leading Change

Culture change is just one of the many changes that you will need to lead through. The following are steps to help you do this.

Listen well—When change is imminent you can be tempted to either operate in denial until you're forced to change or rush to make changes to get it over with as soon as possible. Either extreme robs you of the opportunity to listen well. When you need to lead through change, take time to listen. Listen for lessons from history. Listen to fears and concerns. Listen for the reason behind emotions.

Question thoroughly—After you've listened well, begin to ask questions—lots of them—particularly if you're leading change through an issue that is new to you. Whether it be an organization you recently joined or a project that you weren't intimately involved with, asking questions will help you uncover valuable information about sensitivities, key players, historical nuances, etc. Questions will help you better understand the landscape and make more thoughtful decisions.

Evaluate rigorously—Change is challenging. It's tempting to make snap judgments or jump to quick fixes. Take the time and mental energy to evaluate the situation from all angles before hurrying to a decision. As part of your evaluating, seek wise counsel from others who have either led through something similar or who can add helpful perspective.

Decide thoughtfully—Once you've listened, questioned, and evaluated, it's time to make a decision about what to change and how to lead through it. Consider everything you've gleaned in the process so far and thoughtfully decide how to move forward. As a person of faith, prayer is a key part of this step for me.

Direct confidently—Finally, you need to provide a strong, confident direction for change. Your confidence is drawn from the intentional process you've followed and the thoughtful decision you've arrived at. Now you must direct change with the strength of vision and decisive action.

Leading change is not easy, and therefore, it should not be taken lightly. But this is exactly why you are in a position of leadership—to help set the course and lead others toward your mission. Taking the proper time to listen, question, and evaluate before you decide and direct is critical to leading through change in a way that honors those you're leading. Change is emotional and stressful. Taking time for the process equips you to be aware and sensitive while earning trust with those you lead. Additionally, the process builds courage for everyone involved.

Adaptive Leadership

As you've probably picked up throughout this book, while there is a clear process for leading culture, there is also a lot of nuance and discernment required to effectively lead culture. This is what Harvard professors and authors Marty Linsky and Ronald Heifetz call *adaptive leadership*: "the act of mobilizing a group of individuals to handle tough challenges and emerge triumphant in the end."[34]

Adaptive leadership acknowledges the need for leaders to discern a solution when a proven process or technical solution does not suffice. This is much of what we encounter with leading culture. As I shared at the beginning of the book, leading culture requires leadership insights and an actionable plan. We've spent the better part of the book providing a system for you to install in your organization to help build the scaffolding for a healthy culture—that's the plan part of leading culture. The leadership insights side of leading culture is employing leadership principles and skills that are sensitive and responsive to your unique environment. This is the adaptive skill that is essential for leading culture well.

In Linsky and Heifetz's model, there are four main principles:

1. Emotional intelligence

    Emotional intelligence is the ability to recognize your
    own feelings and those of other people. With this
    awareness, an adaptive leader is able to build trust with
    other participants and foster quality relationships.

2. Organizational justice

    Another fundamental principle of adaptive leader-
    ship is fostering a culture of honesty. Adaptive lead-
    ers know the best policies to introduce for the good
    of the organization. They also know the best ways
    to introduce these changes so that people embrace
    them. Adaptive leaders are willing to accommodate
    other peoples' views, hence, assuring them that
    they are valued and respected.

3. Development

    Adaptive leadership entails learning new things.
    If one technique is not yielding desired results,
    an adaptive leader goes out of his or her way to
    discover new strategies that can work. With new
    techniques, both the employees and the company
    at large will experience growth and development.

4. Character

    Adaptive leadership is about having a deep sense
    of character and being transparent and creative.
    Adaptive leaders may not always be right, but they
    earn the respect of those they work with and prac-
    tice what they recommend.[35]

For many relational leaders, this is the part of the process that you have been wrestling with. You know that there is a uniqueness to leading people that can't fully be captured in any system. It's also why you've been reluctant to embrace any system. My hope is that I've convinced you that both are essential as we effectively seek to steward people in pursuit of our mission.

CULTURE TEAM ACTION PLAN

↳ Evaluate the culture engagement funnel. Where are the majority of your staff now? Have you defined the right steps to move your team further down the funnel?

↳ Are you committed to the patience and persistence required to lead culture? Discuss your historic patterns. Do you stick with change management processes, or do you abandon them when it gets challenging? How effectively have you led change, historically?

↳ What will you do differently to patiently yet persistently lead through change?

↳ Review the main principles of adaptive leadership. Which principles are you naturally stronger or weaker in as an organization? How can you be more purposeful to employ these principles as you lead culture?

CLARITY CHECK

	Yes	No
We have visual assets to reflect our values.	☐	☐
We have a plan to onboard our existing team.	☐	☐
We have a strong plan for leading through the change required.	☐	☐

What is the status of our culture playbook? Started, not started, finished? _____

_____

Where do the majority of our staff fall on the culture engagement funnel? _____

_____

Go to culturemattersbook.com/resources for additional resources from this chapter.

10

Equipping Your Leaders

"The single biggest way to impact an organization is to focus on leadership development. There is almost no limit to the potential of an organization that recruits good people, raises them up as leaders and continually develops them."

—John Maxwell[36]

Steve and his team were starting to feel momentum. They had done the work. They had their culture plan. They had shared it with the entire staff who were cautiously hopeful. Now their success would come down to how they led through it, not just in the initial rollout but in the day-to-day interactions that have the greatest effect on the experience each team member has. They recognized that every leader at every level needed to, well, level up.

A few years ago, Barna, a Christian research organization, released a report that said that 82 percent of young adults say that "society is facing a crisis of leadership because there are not enough good leaders right now."[37] As someone who has devoted my life's work to developing leaders, this was a discouraging statistic. Couple that with several decades' worth of data that says that people don't leave jobs, they leave bad bosses, and the picture just continues to get bleaker.

Leadership author and expert John Maxwell is famous for saying, "Everything rises and falls on leadership." That refrain continues to hold true. Great teams and great cultures require great leadership. Gone are the days of mediocre leaders barking orders. Today's leaders must be more skilled and more emotionally savvy than ever before. The current workplace environment offers employees more options and opportunities. No longer bound by geography, they literally have the world at their fingertips and as a result know what great leaders and great cultures look like.

This workplace landscape has elevated the expectations for leaders and, while that might feel like an impossible expectation at times, I believe it's an extraordinary opportunity.

WHAT DO YOU BELIEVE ABOUT LEADERSHIP?

Before we can talk about the skills a leader needs to lead culture, we first must know what we believe about leadership. What commonly happens for most employees is they perform their job well and find themselves promoted to greater responsibility within the organization. This sounds amazing. You're proud of yourself for your career advancement and excited for the additional responsibilities. But what rarely gets considered by the one promoting or the one being promoted is that your core competencies for success will radically change. No longer are you an individual contributor responsible for your work product. You are now a leader of others and are responsible for leading, guiding, coaching, and directing their work. This is a significant shift in responsibilities that is typically underestimated and likely leads to those disconcerting stats I shared at the beginning of the chapter.

I have vivid memories of this shift in my own leadership journey. I remember one particular Thursday afternoon. The busyness of the day was winding down and all I felt was overwhelm. I had barely touched my to-do list. It was nearly the end of the week and I felt like I had nothing to show for it. I plopped myself down in my desk chair feeling defeated and frustrated. As I began thinking back through my week, I recalled several conversations with my team that resulted in helping them make decisions, work through challenges, and move projects forward. As I evaluated the week, I realized that those conversations and interactions were actually my best contribution. My to-do list was minor. My greater and more important work was in supporting my team.

That was the moment that really challenged what I believed about leadership. Leadership as I more specifically address in my book *The 4 Dimensions of Extraordinary Leadership* is not about you or for you. Leadership is about others. Great leaders recognize that when they are in a position of leadership of others, they have the power to change or affect them and that is sacred work. They are investing in them, developing them, coaching them, supporting them in an effort to bring the best out in them for their growth and the good of the organization. This is absolutely one of the greatest honors and privileges of my life!

Leadership is not about you or for you. Leadership is about others.

But what I see over and over again are leaders who keep trying to do the same thing in a different role. They continue to try to be an extraordinary individual contributor in a job that is no longer about their individual contribution. If we want to effectively lead culture, we have to understand that our role as leaders is to serve and support the team we lead. Any other approach is going to leave you frustrated and your team discouraged.

LEADERSHIP DEVELOPMENT AND CULTURE

The health of your team is directly related to how your people managers lead. When my team and I are working with organizations to help them improve their culture, we often find that a major obstacle to improving their culture is the inconsistency of their leaders.

A marketing company in Dallas had me incredibly baffled by the challenges they were experiencing. They were showing all the usual symptoms of a toxic culture:

significant staff turnover, gossip, mistrust. But when we did our staffwide survey, the team indicated a great deal of camaraderie and love for their leaders. The data seemed completely at odds, and so we dug deeper. What we discovered was that while the staff loved and appreciated each other, they had no trust for how their leaders made decisions. While they respected their leaders as individuals, they didn't respect their leadership skills. This finding reinforced what we repeatedly see—too often people are promoted for their competence and likability but are not trained and equipped for leadership responsibility.

When we talk about leadership development as it relates to team culture, there are two key things we need to cover:

1. Developing good people managers
2. Creating development opportunities for all staff

"This is making so much sense," Elizabeth said with equal measure frustration and hope. "We have really good people, but we've promoted them to more responsibility without really equipping them to succeed with these new responsibilities. I think because I'm a student of leadership, I assume these leadership skills come as easily to others as they do for me. I really feel badly that we've put so much on our managers and not supported them better."

Trying to relieve the pressure he could see Elizabeth was putting on herself, Steve said, "I agree with you, Elizabeth . . . the good news is that we're equipped and committed to do something about it. Now we have better understanding, and we'll do better. Let's figure out where to focus first."

DEVELOPING GOOD PEOPLE MANAGERS

There is a fascinating shift that has taken place in the last few decades. Executive leaders used to be the most looked to within their organization for vision, direction, and guidance. Employees today look more to their direct manager for these things. The expectations on managers are perhaps greater than ever. Not only are they responsible for ensuring their team executes on the organization's goals but they are also expected to be career counselors, coaches, and mentors. For many new leaders, this can feel like an impossible expectation.

Organizations that build great cultures recognize they have to develop and support their managers better.

While this is in no way an exhaustive list of leadership skills, here are eight of the most critical skills managers need to demonstrate in order to positively lead culture.

Self-Leadership

The single greatest skill every leader needs is to lead themselves well. Self-leadership is a commitment to consistent growth, discipline, and doing the right thing for the sake of those you lead. Self-leadership is taking responsibility for your growth and development and recognizing what you need to serve and lead others well.

This is a skill that often takes young leaders by surprise. They haven't been conditioned to lead themselves. Every stage in life up until you enter the workforce directs your steps. You parents encourage you to talk, walk, tie your shoes, and learn your ABCs. Our public education system dictates when you begin school and maps the pathway to receiving your high school diploma. National and state laws permit you to get your driver's license at or around sixteen years old and make it legal for you to drink alcohol at age twenty-one. Cultural and/or family expectations dictate going on to college after high school. And after roughly twenty-two years of being told what to do, you enter the workforce, and no one really seems to care what you do next. It's now up to you.

While no one is directly dictating a pathway for growth, there are expectations that you will grow and consequences if you don't. I often hear from young leaders who were overlooked for a promotion. They realize that growth is still necessary but without a clear plan dictated by someone in authority, they don't know where to begin. I also hear from ambitious young leaders who are frustrated that their employers are not making their career pathway clear.

This is perhaps where one of the biggest lessons for leaders emerges: No one else is responsible for your growth and development. You are. While it is amazing if you find yourself in an organization that provides development opportunities, the best leaders learn to assume this responsibility for themselves. They seek out growth opportunities. They determine where their gaps are. They identify their goals for career development, and they look for opportunities to develop the skills they need to achieve their goals.

Here's how this connects to culture: When leaders at all levels take ownership for their growth and development, they are more deeply engaged. They are not waiting for others to direct their work. They are modeling a sense of ownership and commitment. Instead of feeling like they are victims of their circumstances bound by what those in authority direct, they develop a sense of agency that inspires motivation and increases their engagement.

When I know that I am responsible for my growth and development, I'm better empowered to determine if the role that I'm in and the organization I'm a part of is the best place for me to contribute. And when every team member is leading themselves well, engagement and commitment levels go up throughout the organization.

Emotional Intelligence

The superpower of the best leaders is emotional intelligence. We live in a time when much of our work can be replicated by machines and artificial intelligence. But what cannot be reproduced authentically are the people skills historically referred to as "soft skills," meaning the skills required to emotionally connect and interact effectively with others. I believe that no matter how many job functions artificial intelligence replaces, the need for leaders who can relate and respond to humans will be the differentiating behavior.

While the need for emotional intelligence has grown, the development of these skills has decreased. A growing number of young leaders entering the workforce lack the relational skills that will set them apart in today's workplace. This is why the best organizational cultures focus on cultivating emotional intelligence in all team members.

Emotional intelligence is commonly divided into four categories: self-awareness, self-management, social awareness, and relationship management. In brief, here is how Travis Bradberry and Jean Greaves define these categories in their book *Emotional Intelligence 2.0*:[38]

Self-awareness "is your ability to accurately perceive your own emotions in the moment and understand your tendencies across situations."[39]

Self-management "is your ability to use your awareness of your emotions to stay flexible and direct your behavior positively."[40]

Social awareness "is your ability to accurately pick up on emotions in other people and understand what is really going on with them."[41]

Relationship management "is your ability to use your awareness of your own emotions and those of others to manage interactions successfully."[42]

To build a high-trust culture, you want to seek out team members and promote managers who demonstrate high emotional intelligence. People with strong emotional intelligence have the skills required to successfully lead others as they work through the complexity of everyday organizational life. It is not a culture devoid of tensions, frustrations, or crisis, but a culture where leaders are equipped to know how to appropriately engage these moments and lead everyone forward.

One last note I'll make on this topic is that the power of emotional intelligence is a skill that can be developed. Significant studies show that we are capable of developing these skills and improving them. No matter where or why you may feel like you have weaknesses in one or all of these emotional intelligence competencies, science shows that these are skills we can develop.

Communication

I hold a deep conviction that good communication is an act of respect for others. Even with this strong belief, I fail miserably and frequently when it comes to communicating. Communicating well and consistently is incredibly challenging.

Playwright George Bernard Shaw said, "The single biggest problem in communication is the illusion that it has taken place." Most of us think we are better communicators than we are. To be a good communicator requires intentionality. And when I say "be a good communicator," I'm not referring to public speaking. I'm talking about learning the best practices that allow your everyday interactions to provide the clarity and direction that equips others to succeed.

Inhibitors to good communication:

- Lack of awareness. Oftentimes we're so familiar with the information, we forget that others may be lacking the information.
- Busyness. We're moving so fast that we're not slowing down to consider what needs to be communicated.
- Lack of systems or processes to ensure the right information gets to the right people at the right time.

The heart of good communication comes down to thinking on behalf of others first. This is what great leaders do. Leadership is about serving others, and communicating well is a way that we serve those we lead.

To be a good communicator requires attention to both the *what* and the *how* of communication.

What is the actual information that we need to share.

How is both the practical systems or processes by which we deliver information *and* (often more critically) the emotional intelligence we employ in communicating with others.

Let's take a closer look at these:

What

On any given day a flurry of activity occurs within your team and throughout your organization. Think for a moment about all the decisions you make in a day and all the tasks you accomplish. Now consider how many people were impacted by your decisions and actions. You certainly made decisions and took action, and I'm even more confident that someone else was impacted by those decisions and actions. How did you do? Did you communicate the right information to the right people in a timely manner?

I've found that three simple questions help me be more intentional in my communication:

> Who needs to know?
> What do they need to know?
> When do they need to know it?

These three questions slow you down long enough to think more deliberately about what you're doing and whom it impacts. Great teams recognize that everything they do impacts someone else. There are no lone rangers when we're working on a mission together. Someone somewhere is going to be impacted by a decision you make or an action you take. If you ask yourself these three questions when you're about to make a decision or take action, they will guide you to become a more thoughtful and intentional communicator.

How

The how of communication is twofold. Let's start with the practical side first. You've probably noticed a theme throughout this book that every good culture practice requires a system to support it. The same is true in communication. You need good systems to foster efficient communication. That requires being clear about which tools you use for what type of communication. For example, with the 4Sight team, here are the tools we use and for what purpose:

> Email: nonurgent information sharing
> Asana: project management and task assignment
> Slack: short, quick updates or questions, as well as personal updates and fun stuff
> One-on-one meetings: personal connection, discussions, coaching, feedback
> Team meetings: updates, discussions, and group decisions
> Texts: time-sensitive information
> Phone: sensitive information or when immediate dialogue is necessary

That is certainly not an exhaustive list, but it gives you an idea of how you can improve communication within your team by being clear about the tools you use and what purpose they serve.

The second part of the how has to do with your emotional intelligence in the delivery of information. One of the greatest misunderstandings we have in the Catron house is how we say things to one another. It's rarely *what* we say that creates offense, it's *how* we say it.

Several studies have reinforced what Albert Mehrabian, a researcher of body language, identified. One article states, "He found that communication is 55% nonverbal, 38% vocal, and 7% words only."[43]

Great leaders employ the four categories of emotional intelligence that we discussed earlier in this chapter to ensure that what they say does not get overshadowed or misunderstood by how they say it.

Decision-Making

Does your team understand how you make decisions or is it always a guessing game for them to determine what you will do? I often hear from teams that they don't understand how decisions are made in their organization. They lack clarity for who has the authority to make what decisions. This often results in complacency. Team members get exhausted by trying to figure it out, which in turn leads to lack of action. At its extreme, finger-pointing and blaming occur as no one takes ownership because they are not sure if the decisions are within their power.

The work you did in chapter seven around organizational clarity is a huge step in also bringing clarity to decision-making. A clear organizational chart with defined roles, responsibilities, and goals should solve many of the questions in regard to who has the authority to make decisions.

Additionally, the values you've defined for your team provide clarity for how you approach decision-making as they are the filters that guide your behavior. If you have a value of collaboration, most of your decision-making probably occurs in teams rather than with the authority of an individual.

To clarify decision-making for your team, use the work you did in creating organizational clarity to define your decision-making process. Then reflect on decisions you've recently made and determine how predictable your decision was for others. Did your decision make sense? Was it in alignment with your purpose and goals?

There are several different tools for decision-making, including Gradients of Agreement, Decision-making matrix, the 4Ds from Predictable Success, etc. The style of your leaders, the life cycle of your organization, and other factors may play a part in determining how decisions are made. The important part of decision-making as it impacts culture is that your team understands how decisions are made. They should not be left guessing.

Delegation

Leaders empower others by delegating. The problem with delegation is that most leaders approach it from two extreme and unhelpful perspectives:

1. They delegate to get stuff off their own plate. Essentially, it's all about them as a leader and what they can get rid of.

2. They are afraid to delegate because they aren't comfortable asking others to do things.

Delegating well requires a better perspective on the purpose of delegating. Delegating serves two very important purposes:

1. It creates an opportunity to grow the skills of your team members, fostering an environment for coaching and developing.

2. It forces you to consider what you need to let go of (delegate to others) to make room for the new responsibilities you need to take on and grow from.

Delegating done well allows team members at every level to continue to increase their capacity and skill set.

As with much of what we've named so far, your organizational clarity work will do the heavy lifting in helping you define what needs to be delegated. But beyond that, you want to be looking for opportunities to grow the skills and capacity of your team by delegating projects that will stretch them.

A tool that I use in my coaching work with leaders is something I simply call Only/Could/Must. To start this exercise, create three columns on a spreadsheet, whiteboard, piece of paper, whatever brainstorming method of choice you prefer, and label the columns from left to right: Only I Can Do / I Do but Could Delegate / I Must Delegate.

In each of these columns you're taking inventory of what you currently do and identifying the following:

- Column 1: The things that only you can do. These are the responsibilities that are core to your job. For example, at 4Sight only I can set the vision and direction for the organization. This column is an opportunity for you to get really honest about where your best energy and efforts need to be directed.

- Column 2: The middle column is where you identify the things that you currently do but you could delegate in the near future. Maybe there is a team member you're developing, and you see a pathway to delegate a project to them, or perhaps you have a new hire on the horizon that you'll be able to delegate some work to. The purpose of this column is to help you pay attention to tasks and responsibilities that eventually need to move off your plate to give you more margin for the items in the first column.

- Column 3: The third column is the list that should embarrass you slightly. These are the pet projects or the tasks that you hold on to because you're just too stubborn or controlling to release them. In truth, these are often low-level tasks that make us feel like we've at least gotten something checked off our list today. It might be things like booking travel or checking email, even though you have an assistant that can help you with these things. This is the list you have to get brutally honest about because if you really want the margin to give your best energy to things in the first column, you *must* delegate the items in this one.

The power of this three-column activity is that it gives you visibility and vision for making delegating a normal part of your leadership. If every team member at every level is creating this list, everyone is making space to receive items from someone else's list. If we want a culture where leaders are being continually grown and developed, we have to create a culture where continual growth of adding and releasing work is a normal part of our rhythms.

Accountability

In my twenty-five years of leadership, I've noticed a decline in accountability—both in employees being accountable for their responsibilities and for managers holding their team accountable for those responsibilities. I suspect there are various contributors to this but one that stands out to me is the overcriticism of management. Decades of leadership material has criticized management while elevating leadership. This would be fine if leadership were not disproportionately portrayed as gregarious and relational while undervaluing the discipline and diligence great leaders employ to direct and manage their teams.

By definition, *accountability* means, "an obligation or willingness to accept responsibility or to account for one's actions."[44] The best teams embrace a culture of accountability. Each team member accepts responsibility for their role, and they understand that they will be expected to account for their actions.

You can see why our earlier work matters so much here. When team members lack clarity for their role and their responsibilities, it becomes quite difficult for them to be accountable; they don't understand what they're accountable for. As a result, they are often complacent or disengaged. They might deflect responsibility, claiming, "I didn't know that was my responsibility" or "I thought someone else was doing that."

Accountability is only possible when organizational clarity has been provided. Where accountability goes wrong and gets labeled micromanagement is when accountability isn't accompanied by ongoing conversations that clarify expectations. One of my favorite tools for creating a culture of accountability is the simple question, Who is doing what by when? This simple question provides immense clarity. Whether it's a one-on-one conversation or a team meeting, when team members leave the room clear on who is doing what by when they know what is expected of them and are clear on their contributions. When they don't meet the expectation in that agreement, they have less defense when they are held accountable.

Accountability is only possible when organizational clarity has been provided.

Another powerful and important part of healthy teams is peer-to-peer accountability. When everyone on the team has clarity of their responsibilities and who is doing what and by when, peer-to-peer accountability becomes more common. It is also far more productive than a culture that essentially encourages tattling—one team member tells their manager that another team member has not fulfilled an obligation and the manager is then pulled in to referee.

The greater the clarity, the more accountability naturally occurs at all levels of the organization laterally and horizontally.

Feedback

"What's it like to be on the other side of you?" is one of the most powerful questions we can learn to ask. Healthy teams foster a culture of feedback. Feedback is essentially evaluative communication. Remember when I said that communication is an act of respect to others? Feedback, while sometimes more personal and sensitive than standard communication of information, is the ultimate act of respect for those we engage with. Feedback given with a desire to help others grow and improve builds trust and emphasizes care.

Think for a moment about one of your greatest seasons of growth. Odds are that it involved someone giving you feedback at a critical moment. Maybe it was the tennis coach who corrected your serve and, while you felt clumsy for a while, in the long run, your serve got exponentially better and faster. Maybe it was the coworker who alerted you to how your hurriedness makes other team members feel anxious. Feedback given with an intention to help another person get better is invaluable.

Key aspects of quality feedback

When you think about a time that someone gave you some challenging feedback, what caused you to receive their input? To give and receive feedback well, four key aspects are essential.

Relational—Even though it was hard to hear, you likely did so because the person who gave you the feedback was someone you had relationship with. You knew they wanted the best for you.

Positive and constructive—I bet you can count multiple times that person also gave you positive feedback. Their investment in providing positive feedback gave them credibility to also deliver constructive feedback.

Consistent—Their feedback was also consistent. They didn't just swoop in during the good times or the bad. They were consistently engaged in your work and their feedback demonstrated an ongoing commitment to you. Leaders who provide feedback well consistently use one-on-one meetings, performance reviews, and other organizational systems to provide a consistent and predictable rhythm for giving feedback.

Thoughtful—They employed emotional intelligence in how and when they shared feedback. They were conscious of the setting and the timing to ensure they were giving you feedback in a way that allowed for it to be best received.

Ownership

In great cultures every leader at every level has such a deep commitment to their work, to their team, and to the mission of the organization that they behave like owners. They show up and engage as if they were the founder. They care deeply about the work and demonstrate their commitment through the behaviors we've talked about so far.

Ownership is an attitude rather than a skill, and it's a by-product of development. As you develop your leaders, you increase their buy-in and commitment.

CULTURE TEAM ACTION PLAN

↳ Evaluate the strength of your people managers based upon the eight skills I covered in this chapter (you might have other skills you want to add to the list as well). While this is often a subjective evaluation, what you're trying to identify are the skills that you could better equip your managers with.

Ways to evaluate your managers on these skills:

↳ Rate each manager on a scale of 1 to 5 for each of the eight skills (1 = very weak, 5 = very strong).

↳ Look for patterns across your managers. Are there skills that are weaker for a majority? If so, focus your training efforts for all managers on these weaker areas first.

↳ For each individual manager, have their direct supervisor discuss the eight areas with them. Ask them to self-evaluate and then compare your observations. Celebrate their strong skills and incorporate a plan for their development in their weaker skills as part of your performance review process.

↳ Review your staff survey to see if there are comments that would indicate a gap in the skills of your people managers. Let this information guide your coaching for your managers as well.

CREATING DEVELOPMENT OPPORTUNITIES FOR ALL STAFF

In addition to developing your managers, great cultures focus on development opportunities for their entire team.

Every person on your team is asking, "What's in this for me?" They want to see potential and possibilities in their work. In addition to developing your leaders, you want to be thinking about how you're developing every team member.

One of the challenges that young organizations often face is expectations by team members for promotions. It's not uncommon for employees to equate development with a promotion in title. This presents a challenge when small organizations only have so many manager or director-level positions. Not everyone can be elevated to these titles, but everyone can grow in their current role (which of course is also preparing them for promotions when possible).

The temptation when we begin to talk about creating leadership development programs for all staff is that it quickly begins to feel like an overwhelming system. You may not have the luxury of hiring someone dedicated to this process, and I want to assure you that's not necessary to get started. All you need is one person who is willing to create a simple but consistent way to begin to develop regular rhythms for staff development.

Another thing to note is that team members often have an expectation of development but when pressed they struggle to articulate how they want to grow. Development occurs best when it's owned by the individual but supported by the organization. As you begin to create a regular system for development opportunities and conversations, you'll begin to get a better sense of what employees actually want and need. And you'll begin to see what's serving the organization well.

My advice in this area is this: simple and consistent. Don't feel compelled to overcomplicate it. Start small. Stay consistent. And your development culture will begin to take shape.

CULTURE TEAM
ACTION PLAN

Here are a few simple ideas that you could begin putting in place immediately:

↳ Dedicate one staff meeting per month to leadership development. Brainstorm with other leaders (i.e., executive team or people managers) and make a list of the five to ten core skills that you'd like to focus on for the year ahead.

↳ Find books, TED Talks, online conferences, or other free (or nearly free) resources that you could use for the training of your staff. Then facilitate a discussion with the team around the topic. You might assemble a small team to help you identify resources and facilitate the meetings.

↳ Put it in the budget. You'll never feel like you have the resources to devote to this, so start small and add a little more each year.

↳ Consider fractional leadership support. Many companies (including 4Sight) offer leadership coaches for individuals and entire teams at a fraction of the cost of hiring an in-house leadership development director.

CLARITY CHECK

	Yes	No
We have a good pulse on the strengths and weaknesses of our people managers.	☐	☐
We have a plan for ongoing development of our people managers.	☐	☐
We have a plan for the ongoing development of all our staff.	☐	☐

Go to culturemattersbook.com/resources for additional resources from this chapter.

PHASE 5

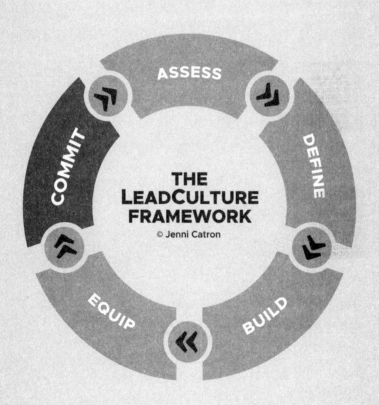

11

Maintaining Momentum

"The only thing of real importance that
leaders do is to create and manage culture."
—Edgar Schein[45]

How do we protect our work?" I had returned to spend a
day with Steve and his Culture Team, and these were
the first words out of their mouth. They were so proud of
the work they had done as a team. They had rolled out the
plan to the entire staff, they had implemented some training for the leaders and the staff, and now they were really
fearful of something knocking them off course. The pain of
culture drift was still familiar, and they were more committed than ever to protecting it. We spent the rest of our day
together talking about the final phase of our work: commit.

MAINTAINING MOMENTUM

I once had a mentor tell me that one of the most important things a leader is responsible for is protecting momentum. I've returned to this nugget of wisdom time and time again. Protecting momentum applies in every area of leadership and it's especially true of your culture. Once you have your culture moving in the right direction, you need to fiercely protect that momentum.

Momentum can be deceiving. When you have it, you think you always will and therefore it's easy to become complacent. You may overlook underlying issues, coasting along until you hit a roadblock. Only then do you realize the fragility of your momentum.

When you don't have it, you feel like you'll never get it, and you're tempted to blame strategies or external circumstances. You grasp at shiny new ideas, oftentimes not realizing that the root cause lies deeper.

One of the most important things a leader is responsible for is protecting momentum.

In Walter Isaacson's biography of Leonardo da Vinci, he explains da Vinci's fascination with momentum: "Leonardo understood the concept of what he called impetus, which is what happens when a force pushes an object and gives it momentum."[46] In typical da Vinci form, he couldn't be content with just the concept; he proved his concept by studying a tightly wound spring, noticing that in the beginning it has greater force but as it unwinds it has less and less power. Da Vinci's meticulous observations reveal profound insights into the nature of momentum and how we can sustain it.

There are four key things we can do as leaders to protect the momentum we've created for our culture:

1. Anticipate the unwinding.
2. Plan for ongoing effort.
3. Know your driving force.
4. Identify the friction.

Anticipate the Unwinding

Your culture work will launch with a boost of momentum. The Culture Team is engaged and excited. They have just completed some really good, meaningful, and hope-filled work for the future of the team. They have communicated and celebrated the plan with the rollout to the staff. Excitement and engagement are high.

Anticipating the unwinding of momentum is crucial. Just as a tightly wound spring loses its force over time, every organization experiences fluctuations in momentum. Having a plan to mitigate these fluctuations is essential for long-term success.

This is why you built a culture operating system, and this is why you need to remain committed to that system. The energy is going to wane. Regular responsibilities and normal work activity will take over. You and the Culture Team need to anticipate the unwinding and not let it discourage you. You knew this was coming and you're prepared to respond to it. Keep working the plan. Acknowledge the ebbs and flows of energy and make adjustments when needed. Your culture plan is a "working plan" in that you'll quickly discover what produces more energy and engagement and what doesn't. Observe the impact of your ideas and adjust accordingly.

Plan for Ongoing Effort

Another one of da Vinci's observations was that "every movement tends to maintain itself; or rather, every body in motion continues to move so long as the influence of the force that set it in motion is maintained in it."[47] Essentially, he was saying you will maintain momentum as long as you continue to give it attention.

Maintaining momentum in your culture work requires ongoing effort. This is where commitment to your employee journey grid becomes critical. The rhythms you've defined for regular nurturing of your culture help to maintain the momentum of your culture work.

Know Your Driving Force

What is your driving force? There was a reason that you engaged the LeadCulture Framework. Maybe it was high turnover, disengaged or misaligned staff, toxic behavior, or rapid growth that you feared would derail your team. Whatever your reason was for getting serious about your team culture, that was your impetus. It is the driving force that you need to remind yourself of regularly. You'll be tempted to skip some of the work. Your culture will "feel" okay and you'll shortchange some of the systems you've defined. You must keep your driving force in mind to help you stay committed to the work. Staying connected to your original compelling reason for getting serious about your culture is key to maintaining momentum.

Identify the Friction

"What prevents perpetual motion, Leonardo realized, is the inevitable loss of momentum in a system when it rubs against reality."[48]

I love that phrase, "when it rubs against reality." Reality in culture work looks like team members who roll their eyes every time you repeat a value. Reality is that in spite of agreeing on the behaviors that drive your values, team members are going to misbehave from time to time. Reality is a new, well-meaning employee who brings their own interpretation of culture and requires coaching and redirecting. Reality is external forces that create pressure and stress and tempt you to pause or abandon your culture plan.

Identifying sources of friction is a critical aspect of momentum management. Just as friction slows down a moving object, external pressures and internal conflicts can hinder your progress. By pinpointing these obstacles, you can address them head-on and keep your momentum intact.

Momentum is both a gift and a challenge. It's a force that propels us toward our goals but demands constant attention and care. With greater awareness of the principles of momentum, we are better equipped to anticipate changes in momentum and proactively protect it.

Let's take a closer look at specific ways you can protect momentum.

REGULAR RHYTHMS FOR ASSESSMENT

A key component of the commit phase of your culture plan is to regularly assess your culture. You want to frequently come back to the question, "What is true right now?" What's true today is not necessarily what was true six months or a year ago.

Annual Survey

The primary way that you do a regular assessment is by facilitating your culture survey at least annually. You'll recall that when you did the survey at the beginning of the LeadCulture Framework, you were not able to assess for your staff values because they had not been written yet. Now you'll conduct parts one and two of the culture survey. Part one is the key elements in the Culture Hierarchy of Needs and part two will be questions based upon your core values.

With a consistent rhythm of assessing these questions, you'll begin to see your progress year after year. Now you're benchmarking against what you've defined as your culture, and you'll be able to adjust your plans according to the gaps you see in your survey results.

A note of caution: it's not uncommon to see little movement or even a little decline in your culture scores the second time you take the survey. This is typically because the clarity you've provided in defining who you are and how you work together has raised more awareness to gaps or challenges in your current culture.

Another common occurrence is that your staff feel more comfortable being honest about the current culture. They may have been holding back on the first survey because it was new, and they didn't know how their answers would be interpreted and/or used against them. Now that they see you are serious about addressing the issues in the culture, they may actually try to be helpful by being brutally honest about their experience. While this may feel discouraging, honesty from your team is the most valuable asset you have in doing meaningful culture work.

Culture Team Quarterly Reviews

On a quarterly basis, gather the Culture Team together for a ninety-minute meeting to check in and assess the state of your culture. In this meeting:

- Review your culture plan. Check in on progress toward the goals you defined. Are you on target? What roadblocks have you hit? What adjustments do you need to make? Remember that plans can be changed so long as those changes are purposeful. If something is not working or having the effect you hoped for, discuss it as a team and agree on changes that will be more helpful.

- Evaluate the effectiveness and consistency of the activities you defined in the employee journey grid. Are they fun and engaging? Have they become routine and monotonous? Make adjustments as needed to keep these routine reminders engaging.
- Assess your values on the scale from actual to aspirational. 1 = very aspirational, 5 = very true of who you are. Have each team member rate each value and discuss your scores. Determine which values need greater emphasis in the quarter ahead.
- Assess which stage you are in based on the culture engagement funnel.
- Share stories of how you're seeing the staff embrace your desired culture.

Culture Team Annual Reviews

On an annual basis, gather the Culture Team for a full-day review. In this meeting:

- Celebrate the progress you've made. Share stories of how you're seeing the staff embrace your desired culture.
- Review your survey results and identify core issues that need to be further addressed in your culture plan.
- Assess your values on the scale from actual to aspirational. 1 = very aspirational, 5 = very true of who

you are. Have each team member rate each value and discuss your scores. Determine which values need greater emphasis in the year ahead.

- Assess which stage you are in based on the culture engagement funnel.
- Refresh your culture plan. This time you want to do a refresh of the plan rather than a review. Ideally, you've implemented much of what you defined originally and now you want to identify your goals for the next year.

"I feel like we have a really good plan and we've just committed to our quarterly and annual rhythms, but what do we need to be looking out for?" Steve asked. "We've been giving a lot of extra time and energy to building this plan and doing the initial phases of the work, but I think it could be really easy for us to have some blind spots to other things that could impact the culture."

"The mere fact that you're asking the question tells me that your antennae are up and all of you will be much more sensitive to the impact on your culture," I responded. "But let's look at a few more culture busters and culture builders as well as some other inflection points that are key indicators that you may need to rally the team and make some adjustments."

You will encounter trouble spots in your culture. It's not a matter of if, it's when. Every day there are myriad forces pushing on your culture. Every person on your team contributes to the culture, positively or negatively, and outside forces consistently test your culture.

Your job as the culture leader is to anticipate these trouble spots and be prepared to respond to them.

Common culture busters include:

- a team member who routinely violates a value
- not executing your culture plan
- unresolved conflict between team members
- gossip or unproductive negative talk
- managers who don't model the values and/or don't align with your desired culture
- not addressing team members who are out of alignment
- poor communication, especially from leadership
- haphazard change management, especially when it involves employees' roles or responsibilities
- inconsistency in following defined systems
- managers/leaders who violate systems

Common culture builders include:

- celebrating team members who model the values, especially peer-to-peer recognition
- candid and respectful conversations at all levels of the organization
- clear communication
- clarity of roles, responsibilities, and expectations for all team members
- regular feedback throughout the organization
- purposeful meetings
- managers who have been well trained and value the sacred work of leadership

- regular times for connection and celebration
- clear onboarding process for new employees

INFLECTION POINTS

For all your efforts to protect your culture, there will be circumstances that impact it that you can't avoid. Some of these will be the result of necessary decisions you need to make and some of them will be external issues you didn't anticipate. These inflection points will affect your culture and you need to be aware of them to prepare for them. Let's look at a couple of common inflection points:

Crisis

By definition, a crisis is "an emotionally significant event" or "an unstable or crucial time or state of affairs in which a decisive change is impending."[49] Crisis for your organization may come in the form of a team member who has a personal crisis that impacts their ability to contribute at work. Perhaps they have to take an extended leave of absence or leave the organization altogether. Crisis may be a major financial issue that leads to significant budget cuts and downsizing. It may be a regulation change that impacts your business model, causing you to make a change in your strategy. Crisis may be a leader who has a moral failure, and your organization has to pick up the pieces and rebuild trust. It may even be a worldwide pandemic that shuts down operations for a time period and revolutionizes how we work.

It's impossible to predict the type of crisis that your organization will encounter, but it's a pretty safe bet that you'll experience a crisis that will impact your culture. My encouragement to you in these moments is to pay attention to the impact the crisis is having on your team. The challenge here is that you'll be responding to the actual issues of the crisis and will feel like you have little time to attend to the culture. The good news is that healthy cultures typically get stronger through crises because they know how they work together—in good and bad. Your true values that guide you will show up clearly in crisis. If you've instilled the values that define your culture, you'll be able to count on them in difficult times. Lean into the strength of your culture to carry you through the crisis together. Focus on your team and how they are doing. Make sure you're communicating well and equipping them to be on the solution side of the crisis with you.

Unfortunately, for teams that have not done the patient and persistent work of leading culture, crises will often tear them apart. All the more reason that this work is essential.

Leadership Transitions

People are going to leave. Well-loved, long-tenured team members will leave, and it will impact your culture. You might be disappointed or sad, as will your team. Don't ignore the emotion of transitions and, at the same time, don't wallow in it. Our roles within organizations are never permanent and people move on with greater frequency than in the past. This is okay. It's often necessary and it's typically for good reason. What you want to help normalize in your culture is equal parts honor and gratitude for the individual's contribution and celebration and support for their next step. Celebrate when team members are moving on to the next right thing for them and their career journey. Ultimately, we want every person to flourish in their gifts and strengths and sometimes that means they move on to another opportunity.

As we've discussed, every person on the team contributes to the culture, so when key leaders leave, the impact is felt. The more tenure and influence a leader has, the more this is true. Therefore, you must anticipate the impact on the culture. Is this going to be a ripple or a wave and how will you handle it?

CULTURE TEAM ACTION PLAN

↳ When an inflection point like a crisis or leadership transition occurs, assemble the Culture Team to get their perspective. Remember, your view on the culture is limited. You need the perspective of team members throughout the organization to help you understand how these inflection points are impacting the team.

↳ Lean into the observations and insights of the Culture Team and together determine how to support the staff and protect the culture.

Protecting your culture is one of your greatest responsibilities as a leader. In the beginning of this book, I shared
the building blocks for success: purpose, culture, and strategy. I'm willing to bet that you have a regular process for
renewing your purpose and strategy every year. You cast
a vision (purpose) and set goals (strategy) that help you
achieve it. I hope I've compelled you to realize the importance of being purposeful to equip your team. Your team is
the linchpin between your purpose and your strategy. That
same commitment and intentionality is needed for committing to your culture.

CLARITY CHECK

	Yes	No
Our culture is moving in a positive direction.	☐	☐
If we're losing momentum, we know why.	☐	☐
We have a plan for facilitating our annual survey.	☐	☐
We have scheduled quarterly and annual meetings for the Culture Team to do the ongoing work.	☐	☐
We know how we'll address culture busters when we see them.	☐	☐

Go to culturemattersbook.com/resources for additional resources from this chapter.

CONCLUSION
The Impact of Culture

"Company culture is the continuous pursuit of building the best, most talented, and the happiest team we possibly can."
— **Andrew Wilkinson**[50]

A year after I started the work with Steve and his team, I visited them for a follow-up meeting. The contrast from my first visit was stark. When I arrived at the office, there was an energy and camaraderie in the air that was nonexistent the year before. The building felt alive with energy and enthusiasm, whereas the year prior it felt solemn and foreboding. As I walked through the halls, I noticed symbols of their culture everywhere. The sticky statements from their values grid had been designed with fun graphics and were framed on the lobby wall. One hallway had big canvas pictures of the team doing volunteer work together in the community. In the staff break room, a "brag board" had little Post-it Notes where team members had written shout-outs of other staff members who had modeled a value. Everywhere I looked there was evidence of their culture at work.

Not only did they have the visible evidence of their culture, but as I caught up with the Culture Team, I heard even more stories of how their behavior and interaction as a staff had changed. Gossip, which had been a big challenge for them previously, was nearly nonexistent. The team was becoming comfortable asking hard questions and leaders were demonstrating more self-awareness in how they responded to those questions. Because of the clarity they now had in their roles and responsibilities, team members had clearer expectations of one another and were appropriately holding each other accountable for commitments. Meetings typically ended with the question, Who is doing what by when?

The culture they had defined and aspired to a year ago was truly becoming their reality, and I couldn't stop smiling as I spent the day observing their hard work paying off.

WHAT ABOUT THE TOP OF THE HIERARCHY?

Perhaps you've noticed that we haven't come back to the top three levels of the Culture Hierarchy of Needs. The reason for this is that the work you've done with the LeadCulture Framework has been setting the stage for these upper levels of the hierarchy to be an overflow of your investment. As leaders, we naturally want people to have a sense of safety, connection, and fulfillment in their work. However, we often lack an understanding of the organizational clarity that we need to provide that establishes the foundation of trust for these things to be realized. Remember our relationship between clarity and trust that we discussed in chapter 2? As you've worked the process, you've set the foundation for the upper levels of the hierarchy to be realized as well.

Let's look at these more closely.

Psychological Safety

In simple terms, this level of the hierarchy is about trust and respect. With the clarity you've provided around your mission, vision, goals, org structure, roles, and responsibilities, you have built trust with your team, and you've earned respect in the process. Team members can now trust what is expected of them and they are equipped to more confidently contribute. This confidence produces an immense sense of safety in a culture. Additionally, you've reinforced this clarity with your employee journey grid by ensuring regular points of feedback through your one-on-one meetings and performance reviews. Finally, you've invested in your people managers better, equipping them to lead with greater awareness of their impact on the culture and the development of the team. All these things contribute to a psychologically safe environment.

Connection

Connection is about employees feeling a sense of belonging. Once again, all your clarity work has instilled a sense of purpose and belonging for their contribution. They understand how their work contributes to the mission, and they know what's expected of them by way of values and behaviors that help them know how to succeed here. Their understanding of how the team is structured and who is responsible for what helps them release fears of competition. They can move beyond silos and more intentionally engage with their coworkers as partners in a shared purpose. As a result, connections and meaningful relationships begin to form. Additionally, the rhythms you've defined for all-staff meetings, staff retreats, and fun days are furthering opportunities to connect and grow together. These interactions are more meaningful and less superficial because of the trust that has been built in the culture.

Fulfillment

Fulfillment is when a team member feels congruence between their personal passions and their work. They are experiencing true meaning and purpose in their work. It's not that every day is a breeze or that they don't have frustrating seasons, but they can quickly reconnect with their purpose and find meaning in the work they do with a team that they trust and respect. This level of the hierarchy is truly an overflow of the others. We can't orchestrate it, but we can set the stage for it, and that is what you've done by working through the LeadCulture Framework.

LEADCULTURE BY-PRODUCTS

What I love most about this work is the long-tail impact it has on culture. Here are a few things I repeatedly see improve in organizations that have committed to the Lead-Culture Framework.

Confidence—It's been stated numerous times, but it can't be undervalued: as you bring clarity to your culture, you build confidence in your team members.

Alignment—Clarity throughout the organization also produces alignment in our efforts. Friction and frustration are less frequent and when those moments occur, team members typically know what needs to happen to realign their efforts.

Ownership—With greater clarity and confidence, team members have a stronger sense of responsibility to the organization and more ownership in the outcomes.

Commitment/Loyalty—Feeling truly a part of the culture, team members are more committed and therefore more loyal to the organization. The level of trust and respect that is fostered goes both ways.

Engagement—Engaged employees are gold! Engaged employees increase profitability, result in less turnover, increase quality of your service or products, have lower absenteeism rates, and are less likely to burn out.[51]

As you continue to work your LeadCulture plan, I suspect you'll find some unexpected by-products of your own to add to this list.

A FEW MORE THOUGHTS

If I had the privilege of sitting down with you for a cup of tea to discuss your culture work, there would be a few more things I would coach you to remember as you do this work.

Be realistic.
Culture shaping takes time. LeadCulture is truly a process, and managing your expectations and the expectations of your team is important. While the culture challenges you're facing feel urgent (and they might be), be realistic about the pace of change.

Be patient and persistent.
You've heard me say this a lot throughout the book, but I'll say it again because I have to remind myself of this *every single day*: leaders are naturally impatient. The very instinct

that helps us see opportunity and cast vision for the future is also the thing that causes us to be impatient and often give up on the process. Resist your instinct to abandon the plan when it feels slow or ineffective. Regroup with your Culture Team, retool some of your efforts if necessary, but don't abandon the plan.

Be clear on your why.
Why do you really care about culture? If it's just a means to get results, it will fall flat. You have to believe it. It has to be more about what you want *for* your team rather than what you want *from* them. Do you really believe that your people are the linchpin for success?

Be honest about the changes you need to make.
As you've worked the process, what perspective shifts have you needed to make to embrace the LeadCulture philosophy? Do you believe that stewardship of people is one of your greatest responsibilities as a leader? Do you recognize that culture work is one of the most valuable and impactful parts of your job?

Remember that leadership shapes human lives—and for that reason it is sacred work. Culture is all about people. It's the uniqueness of each of us contributing to live out a purpose. Slow down to see people and then inspire them to be the best they can be. Everyone wants to be a part of something great—they just need a leader to lead them to it.

Because culture matters!

ACKNOWLEDGMENTS

In some ways this feels like the hardest part of the book to write because so many people have influenced me and the development of the LeadCulture Framework through the years.

I'm particularly grateful for the 4Sight Team for being the biggest cheerleaders (Maddie & Karissa), proofreaders and improvers of the content (Genea, Julie, & Carey), and for being committed to practicing what we preach (our amazing team of coaches). What an honor to do this work with you. I'm so proud of our culture!

Ashley Warren, thank you for always believing in me and helping shape this work from the beginning. Kadi Cole, thank you for challenging me to own my voice as the "Culture Queen." Kenny Jahng, for pushing me to refine the framework. Ali Lopes, for creating all the graphics to bring the framework to life and for knowing what I want better than I do.

To the teams at Maxwell Publishing and Forefront Books, thank you for providing a new publishing home. Chad Johnson and Jared Cagle, thank you for believing in me and this content and for welcoming me into the Maxwell Leadership family. Jennifer Gingerich and Jill Smith, thank you for loving what you do and taking such good care of me through the process.

The culture experts who have gone before me, from whose work I've gleaned so much and whose ideas have influenced mine.

To my husband, Merlyn, who endured another season of book writing, thank you for being the biggest champion of my dreams.

To the amazing leaders and organizations whom I've had the privilege to partner with in facilitating culture work, thank you for trusting me to learn and lead with you. Your stories are woven through these pages, and I know they will inspire so many more leaders and teams to believe that culture matters.

LEADCULTURE RESOURCES

Visit culturemattersbook.com/resources for additional resources to help you implement the LeadCulture Framework.

Prefer to have a LeadCulture Certified Coach guide you through the framework?

LEADCULTURE WORKSHOP

An Onsite Culture Workshop to Unleash Your Team and Accelerate Growth

With our 2-Day intensive workshop, you will be equipped to evaluate, design, and develop the building blocks for an extraordinary culture, and you will leave with a step-by-step process and tools that enable you to create a strategy that allows your organization to thrive.

Here's how it works: A Certified LeadCulture Coach will work with your organization and lead a customized workshop for your team. During the workshop, everyone will learn the trust-building behaviors defined in our culture hierarchy of needs and understand how to engage these behaviors consistently to align your team, accelerate growth, and build unstoppable momentum.

Get more information at get4sight.com/cultureworkshop

LEADCULTURE SURVEY

The LeadCulture Survey is designed to complement the LeadCulture Framework and provide a tool for regular assessment of how your team is doing in reflecting the culture you aspire to.

- 64+ questions
- Built to assess the five levels of the culture hierarchy of needs
- Customized to the client
- Benchmarks against your defined culture rather than against other organizations

Get more information at get4sight.com/survey.

NOTES

1. Bhaswati Roy, "100 Thought-Provoking Company Culture Quotes," *Vantage Circle* (blog), last updated May 15, 2024, https://blog.vantagecircle.com/company-culture-quotes/.

2. Matthew Kelly, *The Culture Solution: A Practical Guide to Building a Dynamic Culture So People Love Coming to Work and Accomplishing Great Things Together!* (North Palm Beach, FL: Blue Sparrow Books, 2019), 10.

3. Daniel Coyle, *The Culture Code: The Secrets of Highly Successful Groups* (New York: Random House, 2018), xx.

4. Dr. Randy Ross, *Relationomics* (Grand Rapids: Baker Books, 2019).

5. Molly Southern, "25 Employee Engagement Statistics You Wouldn't Believe," Oak Engage, last updated July 28, 2023, https://www.oak.com/blog/employee-engagement-statistics/.

6. Roy, "100 Thought-Provoking Company Culture Quotes."

7. Scale Architects, accessed June 6, 2024, https://www.scalearchitects.com/.

8. Lizzie Widdicombe, "The Rise and Fall of WeWork," *New Yorker*, November 6, 2019, https://www.newyorker.com/culture/culture-desk/the-rise-and-fall-of-wework.

9. Kelly, *The Culture Solution*, 40.

10. Saul McLeod, "Maslow's Hierarchy of Needs," Simply Psychology, May 21, 2018, https://canadacollege.edu/dreamers/docs/Maslows-Hierarchy-of-Needs.pdf.

11. Adam Grant, *Think Again: The Power of Knowing What You Don't Know* (New York: Random House, 2021), 209.

12. https://www.gallup.com/workplace/232955/no-employee-benefit-no-one-talking.aspx

13. Anne Marie Chaker, "More Workers Want to Change Jobs, but the Market Is Getting Tougher," *Wall Street Journal*, updated January 22, 2024, https://www.wsj.com/lifestyle/careers/job-search-workers-harder-bd9410c7.

14. Greg McKeown, *Effortless: Make It Easier to Do What Matters Most* (New York: Random House, 2021), 191.

15. Ruth Devine, "20 of the Best Leadership Quotes from Brené Brown," *The CEO Magazine*, August 1, 2019, https://www.theceomagazine.com/business/management-leadership/20-of-the-best-leadership-quotes-from-brene-brown/.

16. Les McKeown, *The Synergist: How to Lead Your Team to Predictable Success* (New York: St. Martin's Press, 2012), 148.

17. 4 Helpful Lists from Paterson StratOp, "What's Happening? Here's 4 Clarifying Questions to Assess Just About Anything," Bridges Coaching, June 8, 2021, https://www.bridgescoaching.net/blog/4-clarifying-questions-to-assess-just-about-anything-tips-tools-series.

18. Kelly, *The Culture Solution*, 148.

19. Kelly, *The Culture Solution*, 56.

20. Laura Hennigan, "15 Mission Statement Examples For Your Business," Forbes Advisor, updated May 31, 2024, https://www.forbes.com/advisor/business/mission-statement-examples/.

21. Jenni Catron, *Clout: Discover and Release Your God-Given Influence* (Nashville: Thomas Nelson, 2014).

22. "37 Company Culture Quotes That Will Inspire Your Team," Spectrio, August 25, 2015, https://www.spectrio.com/internal-communications/37-company-culture-quotes/.

23. Larry Stybel, "Why 33 Percent of Employees Quit in 90 Days," Psychology Today, March 3, 2019, https://www.psychologytoday.com/us/blog/platform-success/201903/why-33-percent-new-employees-quit-in-90-days.

24. Gyöngyvér Martin, "Global Culture Report 2023," HR Lead, December 14, 2022, https://hrlead.at/2022/12/14/2023-global-culture-report/#:~:text=Employees%20want%20more%20from%20work,change%20jobs%20for%20more%20fulfillment.

25. Rob DeSimone, "Improve Work Performance With a Focus on Employee Development," Gallup.com, updated January 19, 2024, https://www.gallup.com/workplace/269405/high-performance-workplaces-differently.aspx.

26. Patty McCord, *Powerful: Building a Culture of Freedom and Responsibility* (Silicon Guild, 2018), xviii.

27. "A Free Assessment to Help You Build an Extraordinary Team," 4Sight Group, accessed June 6, 2024, https://www.get4sight.com/blindspot-assessment.

28. Adam Hayes, "What Was Enron? What Happened and Who Was Responsible," Investopedia, March 1, 2024, https://www.investopedia.com/terms/e/enron.asp.

29. Matt Mayberry, "How to Turn Crisis into Clarity and Ignite Growth," Entrepreneur, June 30, 2017, https://www.entrepreneur.com/leadership/how-to-turn-crisis-into-clarity-and-ignite-growth/296458.

30. James Clear, *Atomic Habits: An Easy & Proven Way to Build Good Habits & Break Bad Ones* (New York: Random House, 2018), 82.

31. Indeed Editorial Team, "36 Quotes About Company Culture to Inspire and Boost Success," Indeed, March 27, 2023, https://uk.indeed.com/career-advice/career-development/quotes-about-company-culture.

32. *Merriam-Webster Dictionary*, s.v. "patient," accessed April 23, 2024, https://www.merriam-webster.com/dictionary/patient.

33. *Merriam-Webster Dictionary*, s.v. "persist," accessed April 28, 2024, https://www.merriam-webster.com/dictionary/persisting.

34. Helen Wale, "Adaptive Leadership," Corporate Finance Institute, October 15, 2023, https://corporatefinanceinstitute.com/resources/management/adaptive-leadership/.

35. Wale, "Adaptive Leadership."

36. John C. Maxwell, "John C. Maxwell on LinkedIn: The Single Biggest Way to Impact an Organization Is to Focus On . . . | 99 Comments," September 9, 2020, https://www.linkedin.com/posts/officialjohnmaxwell_the-single-biggest-way-to-impact-an-organization-activity-6709520968970182656-j-He/.

37. "82% of Young Adults Say Society Is in a Leadership Crisis," Barna Group," October 30, 2019, https://www.barna.com/research/leadership-crisis/.

38. Travis Bradberry and Jean Greaves, *Emotional Intelligence 2.0* (San Diego: TalentSmart, 2009).

39. Bradberry and Greaves, *Emotional Intelligence 2.0*, 24.

40. Bradberry and Greaves, *Emotional Intelligence 2.0*, 32.

41. Bradberry and Greaves, *Emotional Intelligence 2.0*, 38.

42. Bradberry and Greaves, *Emotional Intelligence 2.0*, 44.

43. Jayme Quinn, "How Much of Communication Is Nonverbal? "University of Texas Permian Basin, May 15, 2023, https://online.utpb.edu/about-us/articles/communication/how-much-of-communication-is-nonverbal/.

44. *Merriam-Webster Dictionary*, s.v. "accountability," accessed April 21, 2024, https://www.merriam-webster.com/dictionary/accountability.

45. Smit Nebhwani, "65 Company Culture Quotes for Inspiration, Team Work and Success," DotSignage, accessed January 17, 2024, https://www.dotsignage.com/blog/65-company-culture-quotes.

46. Walter Isaacson, *Leonardo da Vinci* (New York: Simon and Schuster, 2017), 194.

47. Isaacson, *Leonardo da Vinci*, 194.

48. Isaacson, *Leonardo da Vinci*, 196.

49. *Merriam-Webster Dictionary*, s.v. "crisis," accessed April 30, 2024, https://www.merriam-webster.com/dictionary/crisis.

50. Nebhwani, "65 Company Culture Quotes."

51. Kelly, *The Culture Solution*, 10.

4/S THE 4SIGHT GROUP

Are You Ready to Grow Your Leadership and Build an Unstoppable Team?

We Understand That Even Great Leaders Need Great Coaches.

We've helped thousands of leaders build better teams, define a thriving culture, and achieve more success through the implementation of the LeadCulture Framework.

Leadership Coaching • **Culture Consulting**

Visit www.get4sight.com to learn more

4/S THE 4SIGHT GROUP

**LeadCulture Workshops
and Consulting**

Prefer to have a LeadCulture Certified Coach guide you through the LeadCulture Framework?

Visit **www.get4sight.com** to learn more about workshops and customized coaching designed to lead you through the framework.

LeadCulture with Jenni Catron

Powerful interviews.
Practical application.

Subscribe to the **LeadCulture Podcast**
wherever you listen to podcasts.

Visit **podcast.get4sight.com** for
episodes and show notes

THE 4SIGHT GROUP

1:1 COACHING

- Connect With a Coach
- Get Feedback and Support
- Improve Your Leadership

COACHING DELIVERABLES

 A custom coaching plan with measurable actions & a map for success

 Benchmarks for personal and professional development

 Bi-monthly sessions for discussion and support as it relates to your goals and objectives

 Unlimited email correspondence for realtime support

 A committed coach providing regular accountability

Visit **www.get4sight.com**
to learn more

LeadCulture Group Coaching

Join a LeadCulture Group and get exclusive access to:

- Monthly group coaching calls with the cohort of your choice. Choose between our Culture Champion Cohort, our Women in Leadership Cohort and our People Manager Cohort

- Monthly live group training sessions and Q&A with Jenni Catron

- Quarterly live guest expert sessions

- Access to the complete LeadCulture course library

Visit **www.get4sight.com**
to learn more